D1670167

Printed in the USA

Tajik Language:
The Tajik Phrasebook

By Gulshan Ibgragimova

Contents

1. THE BASICS a. Numbers	1. АСОСҲО a. Рақамҳо	1. ASOSHO a. Талаффуз
One (1)	Як (1)	Yak
Two (2)	Ду (2)	Du
Three (3)	Се (3)	Se
Four (4)	Чаҳор (4)/	Chor _char_
Five (5)	Панҷ (5)	Panj _panch_
Six (6)	Шаш (6)	Shash _shut_
Seven (7)	Ҳафт (7)	Haft _sapt_
Eight (8)	Ҳашт (8)	Hasht
Nine (9)	Нуҳ (9)	Nuh
Ten (10)	Даҳ (10)	Dah
Eleven (11)	Ёздаҳ (11)	Yozdah
Twelve (12)	Дувоздаҳ (12)	Duvozdah
Thirteen (13)	Сенздаҳ (13)	Senzdah
Fourteen (14)	Чордаҳ (14)	Chordah
Fifteen (15)	Понздаҳ (15)	Ponzdah
Sixteen (16)	Шонздаҳ (16)	Shonzdah
Seventeen (17)	Ҳабдаҳ (17)	Habdah _haftaa_
Eighteen (18)	Ҳаждаҳ (18)	Hajdah
Nineteen (19)	Нуздаҳ (19)	Nuzdah
Twenty (20)	Бист (20)	Bist _bees_
Thirty (30)	Сӣ (30)	Si
Forty (40)	Чил (40)	Chil
Fifty (50)	Панҷоҳ (50)	Panjoh
Sixty (60)	Шаст (60)	Shast
Seventy (70)	Ҳафтод (70)	Haftod
Eighty (80)	Ҳаштод (80)	Hashtod
Ninety (90)	Навад (90)	Navad
One hundred (100)	Сад (100)	Sad
One thousand (1000)	Ҳазор (1000)	Hazor
Ten thousand (10.000)	Даҳ ҳазор (10,000)	Dah hazor
Fifty thousand (50.000)	Панҷоҳ ҳазор (50,000)	PanjOh hazor
One hundred thousand (100.000)	Сад ҳазор (100,000)	Sad hazor _Shat = Sanskrit_

1

One million (1.000.000)	Як миллион (1.000.000)	Yak milyon (1.000.000)

Ordinal numbers / Рақамҳои тартибӣ / Raqamhoi tartibi

Ordinal numbers	Рақамҳои тартибӣ	Raqamhoi tartibi
First	Якум	Yakum
Second	Дуюм	Duyum
Third	Сеюм	Seyum
Fourth	Чорум	Chorum
Fifth	Панҷум	Panjum
Sixth	Шашум	Shashum
Seventh	Ҳафтум	Haftum
Eighth	Ҳаштум	Hashtum
Ninth	Нуҳум	Nuhum
Tenth	Даҳум	Dahum
Eleventh	Ёздаҳум	Yozdahum
Twelfth	Дувоздаҳум	Duvozdahum
Thirteenth	Сенздаҳум	Senzdahum
Fourteenth	Чордаҳум	Chordahum
Fifteenth	Понздаҳум	Ponzdahum
Sixteenth	Шонздаҳум	Shonzdahum
Sventeenth	Ҳабдаҳум	Habdahum
Eighteenth	Ҳаждаҳум	Hajdahum
Ninteenth	Нуздаҳум	Nuzdahum
Twentieth	Бистум	Bistum

Incomplete amounts / Миқдорҳои нопурра / Mikdorhoi nopurra

Incomplete amounts	Миқдорҳои нопурра	Mikdorhoi nopurra
All	Ҳама	Hama
Half	Нисф	Nisf
A third	Сеяк	Seyak
A quarter	Чоряк	Choryak
A fifth	Панҷяк	Panjyak
A sixth	Шашяк	Shahsyak
A seventh	Ҳафтяк	Haftyak
An eighth	Ҳаштяк	Hashtyak
A ninth	Нуҳяк	Nuhyak
A tenth	Даҳяк	Dahyak

Useful phrases

How much?	Чӣ қадар	Chi qadar
A little	Каме	Kame
Some	Як чанд	Yak chand
A lot	Бисёр	Bisyor
More	Бисёртар	Bisyortar

b. Time & Dates, Tajik Holidays

Days of the week	Рӯзҳои ҳафта	Ruzhoi hafta
Monday	Душанбе	Dushanbe
Tuesday	Сешанбе	Seshanbe
Wednesday	Чоршанбе	Chorshanbe
Thursday	Панҷшанбе	Panjshanbe
Friday	Ҷумъа	Jum'a
Saturday	Шанбе	Shanbe
Sunday	Якшанбе	Yakshanbe

General time

General time	Вақтҳои умумӣ	Vaqthoi Umumi
What time is it?	Соат чанд аст?	Soat chand ast?
It's 6 PM.	Соат 6 аст.	Soat 6 ast.
In the morning	Саҳар	Sahar
In the afternoon	Нисфирӯзӣ	Nisfiruzi
In the evening	Бегоҳӣ	Begohi
Fifteen minutes till 6	Понздаҳ то кам 6	Ponzdah to kam 6
10 minutes till 6	10 то кам 6	10 to kam 6
Today	Имрӯз	Imruz
Yesterday	Дирӯз	Diruz
Now	Ҳозир	Hozir
Tonight	Имшаб	Imshab
In the morning	Саҳар	Sahar
In the evening	Бегоҳӣ	Begohi
In the afternoon	Нисфирӯзӣ	Nisfiruzi
This Tuesday	Ҳамин Сешанбе	Hamin Seshanbe
This week	Ҳамин ҳафта	Hamin hafta
This month	Ҳамин моҳ	Hamin moh

This year	Ҳамин сол	Hamin sol
Tomorrow morning	Пагоҳ/фардо саҳар	Pagoh/fardo sahar
Tomorrow afternoon	Пагоҳ / фардо нисфирӯзӣ	Pagoh /fardo nisfiruzi
Tomorrow evening	Пагоҳ / фардо бегоҳӣ	Pagoh /fardo begohi
Yesterday morning	Дирӯз саҳар	Diruz sahar
Yesterday afternoon	Дирӯз нисфирӯзӣ	Diruz nisfiruzi
Yesterday evening	Дирӯз бегоҳӣ	Diruz begohi

Tajik holidays

Christmas	Мавлуди Исо	Mavludi Iso
Nowruz	Наврӯз	Novruz
Natinal Unity Day	Рӯзи ваҳдати миллӣ	Ruzi vahdati milli
Independence Day September 9	Рӯзи Истиқлолияти	Ruzi istiqloliyati

Months	**Моҳ**	**Moh**
January	Январ	Yanvar
February	Феврал	Fevral
March	Март	Mart
April	Апрел	Aprel
May	Май	Mai
June	Июн	Iyun
July	Июл	Iyul
August	Август	Avgust
September	Сентябр	Sentyabr
October	Октябр	Oktyabr
November	Ноябр	Noyabr
December	Декабр	Dekabr
What date is today?	Имрӯз чандум аст?	Imruz chandum ast?

c. Customs	**Гумрук**	**Gumruk**
Q: Do you have something to declare?	Оё шумо чизе барои эълон кардан доред?	Oyo shumo chize baroi e'lon kardan dored ?

4

A: I have something to declare	Ман чизе барои эълон кардан дорам	Man chize baroi e'lon kardan doram
A: I have ... to declare	Ман..... барои эълон кардан дорам	Man ..... baroi e'lon kardan doram
A: I have nothing to declare	Ман чизе барои эълон кардан надорам	Man chize baroi e'lon kardan nadoram
I will be in Tajikistan for ... days	Ман дар Тоҷикистон..... рӯз боқӣ мемонам	Man dar Tojikiston ..... ruz boqi memonam
I wil be staying at ...	Ман дар..... меистам.	Man dar ..... meistam
I'm a tourist	Ман сайёҳ мебошам	Man sayyoh mebosham
I'm doing business in Tajikistan	Ман дар Тоҷикистон соҳибкорам	Man dar Tojikiston sohibkoram
Do you speak English?	Шумо бо забони англисӣ гап мезанед?	Shumo во zaboni anglisi gap mezaned ?
I don't understand	Ман намефаҳмам	Man namefahmam
I'm sorry	Мутаассифам	Mutaassifam
Q: Where did you arrive from?	С: Шумо аз куҷо омадед?	S : Shumo az kujo omaded ?
A: I arrived from ...	Ҷ: Ман аз..... омадам	Ç : Man az ..... omadam
Q: How long will you be here?	С: Шумо чӣ қадар дар инҷо меистед?	S : Shumo chi qadar dar injo meisted ?
A: I will be here for ... days	Ҷ: Ман дар инҷо..... рӯз меистам	Ç : Man dar injo..... ruz meistam
CUSTOMS VOCABULARY BANK	ЛУҒАТИ ГУМРУК	LUGHATI GUMRUK
Passport	Шиноснома	Shinosnoma
Ticket	Чипта	Chipta
Baggage claim check	Қабули боғоҷ	Qabuli boghoj
Immigration	Муҳоҷират	Muhojirat
Passport control	Назорати шиноснома	Nazorati shinosnoma

d. Getting Around/Transport	Ҳаракат/Нақлиёт	Harakat/Haqliyot
VOCAB BANK	Луғат	Lughat
BUS	Автобус	Avtobus
Where is the bus stop?	Истгоҳ дар кучо аст?	Istgoh dar kujo ast?
When is the next stop?	Истогоҳи оянда кай аст?	Istogohi oyanda kay ast?
When is the next bus?	Автобуси оянда кай мешавад?	Avtobusi oyanda kay meshavad?
When is the last bus?	Автобуси охирин кай мешавад?	Avtobusi ohirin kay meshavad?
Does this bus go to ...	Оё ин автобус ба... меравад?	Oyo in avtobus ba... meravad?
Is this seat taken?	Оё ин ҷой машғул аст?	Oyo in joy mashghul ast?
How much is it?	Чанд пул аст?	Chand pul ast?
Where can I buy a ticket?	Ман аз кучо чипта харидорй карда метавонам?	Man az kujo chipta kharidori karda metavonam?
One ticket please.	Лутфан, як чипта диҳед.	Lutfan, yak chipta dihed.
Two tickets please	Лутфан, ду чипта диҳед.	Lutfan, du chipta dihed.
Three tickets please	Лутфан, се чипта диҳед.	Lutfan, se chipta dihed.
Four tickets please	Лутфан, чор чипта диҳед.	Lutfan, chor chipta dihed
TAXI	ТАКСИ	TAKSI
Where can I get a taxi?	Ман кучо такси гирифта метавонам?	Man kujo taksi girifta metavonam?
I need a taxi.	Ба ман такси лозим аст.	Ba man taksi lozim ast.
How much is it?	Чанд пул аст?	Chand pul ast?

Please drive me to this address.	Лутфан, маро ба ин суроға бурда расонед.	Lutfan, maro ba in surogha burda rasoned.
Please stop here.	Лутфан, дар инҷо истед.	Lutfan, dar injo isted.
I need to get out.	Ман бояд фароям.	Man boyad faroyam.

e. Hotels	**Меҳмонхонаҳо**	**Mehmonhonaho**
BOOKING IN ADVANCE	Брони пешакӣ	Broni peshaki
Do you have a room?	Оё шумо утоқ доред?	Oyo shumo utoq dored?
How much is it per night?	Як шабаш чанд пул аст?	Yak shabash chand pul ast?
Does it include Internet?	Оё Интернет ба ин дохил мешавад?	Oyo Internet ba in dohil meshavad?
How much is Internet access?	Интернет чанд пул аст?	Internet chand pul ast?
Is the Internet fast?	Оё интернети босуръат аст?	Oyo interneti bosur'at ast?
I need one bed	Ба ман як кат лозим	Ba man yak kat lozim
I need two beds	Ба ман ду кат лозим аст	Ba man du kat lozim ast
It's for...	Ин барои..... аст	In baroi..... ast
...one person	.... як нафар	.... yak nafar
...two people	...ду нафар	...du nafar
...three people	...се нафар	...se nafar
...four people	... чор нафар	... chor nafar
... five people	...панҷ нафар	...panj nafar
... six people	...шаш нафар	...shash nafar
I'd like to see the room, please	Лутфан, ба ман утоқро нишон диҳед	Lutfan, ba man utoqro nishon dihed
Could we do a lower price, please?	Оё ин арзонтар мешавад?	Oyo in arzontar meshavad?
Can I see another room?	Метавонам, ки дигар утоқро бинам?	Metavonam, ki digar utoqro binam?

7

Is there a deposit?	Оё ҷои амонатгузорӣ ҳаст?	Oyo joi amonatguzori hast?
Yes, I'll take it.	Ҳа, ман онро мегирам.	Ha, man onro megiram.
No, I wont take it.	Не, ман онро намегирам.	Ne, man onro namegiram.
What time is check in?	Баҳайдгирӣ соати чанд аст?	Baqaydgiri soati chand ast?
What time is check out?	Хориҷшавӣ аз меҳмонхона соати чанд аст?	Xorijshavi az mehmonhona soati chand ast?
Does it include breakfast?	Оё наҳориро дар бар мегирад?	Oyo nahoriro dar bar megirad?
What time is breakfast?	Соати чанд наҳорӣ аст?	Soati chand nahori ast?
I need to be woken up at 6AM	Лутфан, маро соати 6 аз хоб бедор кунед	Lutfan, maro soati 6 az khob bedor kuned
Is there a laundry?	Оё ҷомашӯй ҳаст?	Oyo jomashui hast?
Is there a swimming pool?	Оё ҳавзи шиноварӣ ҳаст?	Oyo havzi shinovari hast?
Is there a safe?	Оё сейф ҳаст?	Oyo seyf hast?
Where can I change money?	Дар куҷо пул иваз карда метавонам.	Dar kujo pul ivaz karda metavonam.
Can I buy a tour?	Оё ман метавонам, ки чипта барои саёҳат кардан харидорӣ намоям.	Oyo man metavonam, ki chipta baroi sayohat kardan kharidori namoyam.
What time is checkout?	Хориҷшавӣ аз меҳмонхона соати чанд аст?	Horijshavi az mehmonhona soati chand ast?
I need a taxi for 8AM, please.	Дар соати 8 ба ман такси лозим мешавад.	Dar soati 8 ba man taksi lozim meshavad.
I'm leaving at ...	Ман соати... тарк мекунам	Man soati... tark mekunam

I need to leave my bags here.	Ман бояд бағочи худро дар инчо бигзорам.	Man boyad baghoji khudro dar injo bigzoram.
Thank you very much!	Ташаккури зиёд!	Tashakkuri ziyod!
PROBLEMS:	МУШКИЛОТ:	MUSHKILOT:
The bill is incorrect	Ҳисоб хато аст	Hisob khato ast
I need a new key	Ба ман калиди нав лозим аст	Ba man kalidi nav lozim ast
I need a blanket	Ба ман курпа лозим аст	Ba man kurpa lozim ast
I need a receipt	Ба ман расид лозим аст	Ba man rasid lozim ast
The toilet is broken	Ҳоҷтхона кор намекунад	Hojthona kor namekunad
The TV is broken	Телевизор кор намекунад	Televizor kor namekunad
It's too hot	Хеле гарм аст	Hele garm ast गरम
It's too cold	Хеле хунук аст	Hele khunuk ast
It's too noisy	Хеле пурғавғо аст	Hele purghavgho ast
The room is dirty	Ҳуҷра ифлос аст	Hujra iflos ast
VOCAB BANK	ЛУҒАТ	LUGHAT
Hotel	Меҳмонхона	Mehmonhona मेहमान
Motel	Меҳмонхона	Mehmonhona
Hostel	Хобгоҳ	Hobgoh
Apartment	Хона	Hona
Inexpensive	Арзон	Arzon

f. Directions	Самтҳо	Samtho
Excuse me, where is ...	Бубахшед, ... дар кучо аст?	Bubahshed, ... dar kujo ast?
Could you show me where to go?	Лутфан, ба ман нишон диҳед, ки ба кучо равам	Lutfan, ba man nishon dihed, ki ba kujo ravam
Which street is it on?	Дар кадом кӯча чойгир аст?	Dar kadom kucha joygir ast?

9

What is the address?	Суроғаи он чист?	Suroghai on chist?
Can I get there ...	Оё ман ба онҷо рафта метавонам...	Oyo man ba onjo rafta metavonam...
... by foot	.... пиёда	.... piyoda
... by train	.... бо қаттора	.... bo qattora
... by car	...бо мошин	... bo moshin
... by bus	...бо автобус	... bo avtobus
To the right	Ба тарафи рост	Ba tarafi rost
To the left	Ба тарафи чап	Ba tarafi cap
At the corner	Дар канор	Dar kanor
Straight ahead	Рост	Rost
Next to	Дар бари	Dar bari
In front of	Дар пеши	Dar peshi
Behind	Дар қафо	Dar qafo
Is it far?	Дур аст?	Dur ast?
Is it nearby?	Наздик аст?	Nazdik ast?
How do I get there?	Чӣ тавр ба онҷо равам?	Chi tavr ba onjo ravam?
Do you know?	Оё шумо медонед?	Oyo shumo medoned?
I'm sorry, I only speak a little Tajik	Мутаассифам, ман бо забони тоҷик кам гап мезанам	Mutaassifam, man bo zaboni tojik kam gap mezanam
VOCAB BANK	ЛУҒАТ	LUGHAT
Street	Кӯча	Kucha
Building	Бино	Bino
Boulevard	Кӯчабоғ	Kuchabogh
City	Шаҳр	Shahr
Square	Майдон	Maydon
Neighborhood	Гирду атроф/ҳамсоягӣ	Girdu atrof/hamsoyagi

g. Shopping	Харид	Harid
Where is the store?	Мағоза дар куҷо аст?	Maghoza dar kujo ast?
Where is the supermarket?	Супермаркет дар куҷо аст?	Supermarket dar kujo ast?

10

Where is the mall?	Фурӯшгоҳ/маркази савдо дар кучо аст?	Furushgoh/markazi savdo dar kujo ast?
Where is the grocery store?	Мағозаи хӯроквори дар кучо аст?	Maghozai khurokvori dar kujo ast?
Where is the bookstore?	Мағозаи китоб дар кучо аст?	Maghozai kitob dar kujo ast?
I'm looking for this book.	Ман дар ҷустуҷӯи ин китоб ҳастам.	Man dar justujui in kitob hastam.
I need a newspaper.	Ба ман маҷалла лозим аст	Ba man majalla lozim ast
Q: Can I help you?	С: Ба шумо чӣ тавр ёрӣ расонида метавонам?	S: Ba shumo chi tavr yori rasonida metavonam?
A: We don't have it.	Ҷ: Мо инро надорем.	Ç: Mo inro nadorem.
I need your help	Ба ман кӯмаки шумо лозим аст	Ba man kumaki shumo lozim ast
Where can I buy?	Аз кучо харидорӣ карда метавонам?	Az kujo kharidori karda metavonam?
I need to buy ...	Ман бояд... харидорӣ намоям	Man boyad... kharidori namoyam
Could I try this on?	Оё ман инро барои санҷиш пӯшида метавонам	Oyo man inro baroi sanjish pushida metavonam
My size is ...	Андозаи ман.... аст	Andozai man.... ast
How much is this?	Чанд пул аст?	Chand pul ast?
Please write the price down on a piece of paper	Лутфан, нархи онро дар қоғаз нависед	Lutfan, narhi onro dar qoghaz navised
I'm just looking	Ман танҳо нигоҳ дорам	Man tanho nigoh doram
This is too expensive	Ин хеле гарон аст	In khele garon ast
Can we lower the price?	Арзонтар мешавад?	Arzontar meshavad?
Do you take credit cards?	Оё шумо корти плостикӣ қабул мекунед?	Oyo shumo korti plostiki qabul mekuned?

11

I will take that.	Ман онро мегирам	Man onro megiram
I need receipt, please	Лутфан, ба ман расид диҳед	Lutfan, ba man rasid dihed
It's broken	Ин вайрон аст	In vayron ast
I need a refund	Маблағро баргардонед	Mablaghro bargardoned
I need to return this	Ман бояд инро бозпас намоям	Man boyad inro bozpas namoyam तायं
I need a bag	Ба ман сумка лозим аз	Ba man sumka lozim az
I don't need a bag	Ба ман сумка лозим нест	Ba man sumka lozim nest
VOCAB BANK	ЛУҒАТ	LUGHAT
Men's Restroom	Ҳоҷатхона барои мардон	Hojathona baroi mardon
Women's Restroom	Ҳоҷатхона барои занон	Hojathona baroi zanon
Restroom	Ҳоҷатхона	Hojathona शौन
Do Not Enter	Даромадан манъ аст	Daromadan man' ast
No Smoking	Тамоку кашидан манъ аст	Tamoku kashidan man' ast
Information	Маълумот	Ma'lumot माहूमात
Open	Кушода	Kushoda
Closed	Пӯшида	Pushida
No Cameras	Истифодаи камера манъ аст	Istifodai kamera man' ast मना
No Cell Phone Use	Истифодаи телефони мобилй манъ аст	Istifodai telefoni mobili man' ast

h. At the bank   Дар бонк   Dar bonk

Where is the bank?	Бонк дар куҷо аст?	Bonk dar kujo ast?
What time does the bank open?	Соати чанд бонк кушода мешавад?	Soati chand bonk kushoda meshavad?
What time does the bank close?	Соати чанд бонк пӯшида мешавад?	Soati chand bonk pushida meshavad?

12

I don't remember my pin	Ман рамзи пин-и худро дар хотир надорам	Man ramzi pin-i khudro dar khotir nadoram
Here is my card.	Марҳамат, корти ман	Marhamat, korti man
I need to exchange money	Ман бояд пул иваз намоям	Man boyad pul ivaz namoyam
I need to withdraw money	Ман бояд пул гирам	Man boyad pul giram
What is the price?	Нархаш чӣ қадар аст?	Narhash chi qadar ast?
What is the exchange rate?	Қурби пул чӣ қадар аст?	Qurbi pul chi qadar ast?
I need to find an ATM	Ба ман банкомат лозим аст	Ba man bankomat lozim ast
Smaller notes, please	Лутфан, асъори хурдтар диҳед	Lutfan, as'ori khurdtar dihed
Do you accept traveler's check?	Оё шумо чеки мусофирро қабул мекунед?	Oyo shumo cheki musofirro qabul mekuned?
Do you accept credit cards?	Шумо корти плостикӣ қабул мекунед?	Shumo korti plostiki qabul mekuned?
Do I need to sign?	Имзо кардан шарт аст?	Imzo kardan shart ast?
I need the receipt, please	Лутфан, ба ман расид диҳед	Lutfan, ba man rasid dihed

i. Internet	**Интернет**	**Internet**
Do you have free Internet?	Шумо Интернети ройгон доред?	Shumo Interneti roygon dored?
Where is an Internet café?	Дар куҷо интернет - кафе ҳаст?	Dar kujo internet-kafe hast?
How much does it cost to access the Internet?	Дастрасӣ ба интернет чанд пул аст?	Dastrasi ba internet chand pul ast?
Is this a high speed connection?	Оё суръаташ баланд аст?	Oyo sur'atash baland ast?

What is the password?	Гузарвожааш (паролаш) чист?	Guzarvozhaash (parolash) chist?
Which network do I connect to?	Ба кадом шабака пайваст шавам?	Ba kadom shabaka payvast shavam?
Is it wireless Internet?	Оё ин Интернети бесим аст?	Oyo in Interneti besim ast?
How much does it cost?	Чӣ қадар арзиш дорад?	Chi qadar arzish dorad?
How do I log on?	Чӣ тавр ворид шавам?	Chi tavr vorid shavam?
Connection is dead	Пайвастшавӣ номумкин аст	Payvastshavi nomumkin ast
The computer is not working	Компютер кор накарда истодааст	Kompyuter kor nakarda istodaast
I'm done using the Internet.	Ба бо Интернет коркарданро анҷом додам	Ba bo Internet korkardanro anjom dodam
I need to ...	Ман бояд...	Man boyad...
... check my email	... почтаро санҷидан	... pochtaro sanjidan
... use Skype	...аз Skype истифода бурдан	...az Skaip istifoda burdan
... print out documents	...ҳуҷҷатҳоро чоп кардан	...hujjathoro chop kardan
... scan documents	... ҳуҷҷатҳоро скан кардан	... hujjathoro skan kardan

j. Cell Phone	**Телефони мобилӣ**	**Telefoni mobili**
I'd like to buy a cell phone.	Ман мехоҳам, ки телефони мобилӣ харидорӣ намоям	Man mehoham , ki telefoni mobili kharidori namoyam
I need a cell phone charger	Ба ман барқфизо лозим аст	Ba man barqfizo lozim ast
My number is ...	Рақами ман... мебошад	Raqami man meboshad ...
What is your phone number?	Рақами шумо чанд аст?	Raqami shumo chand ast ?

14

| I need to speak to ... | Ман бояд бо.... гап занам | Man boyad bo .... gap zanam |
| What is the code for ... | Рамзи... чанд аст? | Ramzi ... chand ast ? |

k. Post office

k. **Post office**	Почта	Pochta
Where is the post office?	Почта дар куҷо аст?	Pochta dar kujo ast ?
I need to send ...	Ман бояд... ирсол намоям	Man boyad ... irsol namoyam
... A domestic package	... марсулаи дохилӣ	... marsulai dohili
... an international package	...марсулаи байналмилалӣ	... marsulai baynalmilali
... a postcard	...қоғази хатнависӣ	... qoghazi khatnavisi
... a parcel	...пакет	... paket
Postal code	Рамзи почта	Ramzi pochta
Declaration	Эъломия	E'lomiya
Stamp	Маркаи почта	Markai pochta

l. Business

l. **Business**	Соҳибкорӣ/Кор	Sohibkori/Kor
I'm here on business	Ман дар инҷо бо як кор қарор дорам	Man dar injo bo yak kor qaror doram
I'm from ...	Ман аз ... мебошам	Man az mebosham ...
... America	...Америка	... Amerika
... England	...Инглистон	... Ingliston
Could I have your business card?	Метавонам, ки корти кории шумор гирам?	Metavonam, ki korti korii shumor giram?
Here is my business card	Марҳамат, корти кории ман	Marhamat, korti korii man
Where is the conference?	Конфронс дар куҷо аст?	Konfrons dar kujo ast?
Where is the company office?	Идораи ширкат дар куҷо аст?	Idorai shirkat dar kujo ast?
Where is the business building?	Бинои корӣ дар куҷо аст?	Binoi kori dar kujo ast?

15

I'm here for a business meeting	Ман дар инҷо вохӯрии корӣ дорам	Man dar injo vohirii kori doram
I'm here for a conference.	Ман дар инҷо дар конфронс иштирок дорам	Man dar injo dar konfrons ishtirok doram
I'm here for a trade show	Ман дар инҷо дар намоиши савдо иштирок мекунам	Man dar injo dar namoishi savdo ishtirok mekunam
Could you translate please?	Лутфан, тарҷума кунед	Lutfan, tarjuma kuned
I need an interpreter.	Ба ман тарҷумон лозим аст	Ba man tarjumon lozim ast
Pleasure doing business with you.	Аз кор кардан бо шумо хушнуд ҳастам	Az kor kardan bo shumo khushnud hastam
That was a great meeting!	Вохӯрии хеле олиҷаноб буд!	Vohurii khele olijanob bud!
That was a great conference!	Конфронси олиҷаноб буд!	Konfronsi olijanob bud!
That was a great trade show!	Намоиши савдои одӣ буд!	Namoishi savdoi odi bud!
Thank you.	Ташаккур	Tashakkur
Should we go out for lunch?	Барои хӯрдани хӯроки нисфирӯзӣ меравем?	Baroi khurdani khuroki nisfiruzi meravem?
Should we go out for dinner?	Барои хӯрдани хӯроки шом меравем?	Baroi khurdani khuroki shom meravem?
Should we go out for a drink?	Барои нӯшидан меравем?	Baroi nushidan meravem?
Here is my email	Марҳамат, почтаи электронии ман	Marhamat, pochtai elektronii man
Here is my phone number	Марҳамат, рақами телефони ман	Marhamat, raqami telefoni man
m. Museums/Tours	**Осорхонаҳо/Саёҳат**	**Osorhonaho/Sayohat**
MUSEUMS	ОСОРХОНАҲО	OSORHONAHO

Where is the museum?	Осорхона дар куҷо аст?	Osorhona dar kujo ast ?
What time does the museum open?	Соати чанд осорхона кушода мешавад?	Soati chand osorhona kushoda meshavad ?
I'd like to hire a guide.	Барои ман роҳбалад лозим аст	Baroi man rohbalad lozim ast
How much does a ticket cost?	Чипта чанд пул аст?	Chipta chand pul ast ?
I need ...	Ба ман...лозим аст	Ba man lozim ast ...
... one ticket	...як чипта	yak chipta ...
... two tickets	...ду чипта	... du chipta
... three tickets	...се чипта	... se chipta
... four tickets	...чор чипта	... chor chipta
TOURS	САЁҲАТ	SAYOHAT
I'd like to ...	Ман мехостам, ки...	Man mehostam , ki ...
... take the day tour	...ба саёҳати якрӯза равам	... ba sayohati yakruza ravam
... take the morning tour	...ба саёҳати саҳар равам	... ba sayohati sahar ravam
... take the evening tour	...ба саёҳати бегоҳӣ равам	... ba sayohati begohi ravam
How long is the tour?	Саёҳат чӣ қадар давом мекунад?	Sayohat chi qadar davom mekunad ?
How much does it cost?	Чӣ қадар арзиш дорад?	Chi qadar arzish dorad ?
Is food included?	Хӯрок дохил аст?	Hurok dohil ast ?
Is there water available?	Оё об ҳаст?	Oyo ob hast ?
What time will we return?	Соати чанд бо бармегардем?	Soati chand bo barmegardem ?

n. Special Need Travelers (Seniors, Children, Disabilities)	Сайёҳони эҳтиёҷманд (Пиронсолон, Кӯдакон, Маъюбон)	Sayyohoni ehtiyojmand (Pironsolon, Kudakon, Ma'yubon)
DISABILITIES/SENIORS	МАЪЮБОН/ПИРОНСОЛОН	MA'YUBON/PIRONSOLON
I need help, please.	Лутфан, ба ман ёрӣ диҳед	Lutfan,ba man yori dihed
Is there an elevator?	Лифт ҳаст?	Lift hast?
How many steps are there?	Чанд қадам аст?	Chand qadam ast?
Could you help me across the street please?	Лутфан, маро аз роҳ гузаронед	Lutfan, maro az roh guzaroned
I have a disability.	Ман маъюб ҳастам	Man ma'yub hastam
I need to sit down, please.	Ман бояд нишинам	Man boyad nishinam
Is there wheelchair access?	Оё курсии чархдор ҳаст?	Oyo kursii charhdor hast?
Are there restrooms for people with disabilities?	Оё ҳоҷатхонаҳои махсус барои маъюбон ҳаст?	Oyo hojathonahoi mahsus baroi ma'yubon hast?
Are guide dogs allowed?	Оё барои сагҳои роҳбалад иҷозат ҳаст?	Oyo baroi saghoi rohbalad ijozat hast?
VOCAB BANK	ЛУҒАТ	LUGHAT
Ramp	Нишебӣ/пастхамӣ	Nishebi/pasthami
Wheelchair	Курсии чархдор	Kursii charhdor
CHILDREN	КӮДАКОН	KUDAKON
I have children.	Ман фарзанддор ҳастам	Man farzanddor hastam
Are children allowed?	Оё барои кӯдакон иҷозат ҳаст?	Oyo baroi kudakon ijozat hast?
Is there a children's menu?	Оё менюи махсус барои кӯдакон ҳаст?	Oyo menyui mahsus baroi kudakon hast?

Is there a baby changing room?	Оё ҳучра барои иваз намудани либоси кӯдак ҳаст?	Oyo hujra baroi ivaz namudani libosi kudak hast?
Is there a baby seat?	Оё ҷой нишаст барои кӯдак ҳаст?	Oyo joy nishast baroi kudak hast?
I need a ...	Ба ман...лозим ҳаст	Ba man...lozim hast
... stroller	...аробачаи бачагона	...arobachai bachagona
... highchair	...курсии баланд барои кӯдакон	...kursii baland baroi kudakon
I need ...	Ба ман...лозим ҳаст	Ba man... lozim hast
... diapers	... уребча	... urebcha
... baby wipes	...сачоқ барои кӯдакон	...sachoq baroi kudakon

2. MEETING PEOPLE

a. Getting Acquainted

2. ВОХӮРӢ БО ОДАМОН

a. Шиносоӣ

2. BOHURI BO ODAMON

a. Shinosoi

Hi, my name is ...	Салом, номи ман...	Salom, nomi man...
Hello	Ва алайкум салом	Va alaikum salom
Good morning	Субҳ ба хайр	Subh ba khayr
Good afternoon	Салом	Salom
Good evening	Шом ба хайр	Shom ba khayr
How are you?	Шумо чӣ хел ҳастед?	Shumo chi khel hasted?
I'm good and you?	Ман хуб ҳастам, шумо чӣ?	Man khub hastam, shumo chi?
My name is ...	Номи ман...	Nomi man...
What is your name?	Номи шумо чист?	Nomi shumo chist?
Nice to meet you	Аз шиносоӣ бо шумо шод ҳастам	Az shinosoi bo shumo shod hastam
I'm from ...	Ман аз	Man az ...
I'm an American	Ман Амрикой мебошам	Man Amrikoi mebosham
I am British	Ман Вритонёй	Man Britonei
Mr.	Ҷаноб	Janob
Mrs.	Хонум	Honum

Ms.	Хонум	Honum
Do you speak English?	Шумо бо забони англисӣ гап мезанед?	Shumo bo zaboni anglisi gap mezaned?
I understand	Ман мефаҳмам	Man mefahmam
I'm sorry, I don't understand	Мутаассифам, ман намефаҳмам	Mutaassifam, man namefahmam
I'm in Tajikistan on business	Ман дар Тоҷикистон кор дорам	Man dar Tojikiston kor doram
I'm in Tajikistan to study	Ман ба Тоҷикистон барои таҳсил омадам	Man ba Tojikiston baroi tahsil omadam
I'm in Tajikistan for a conference	Ман ба инҷо барои иштирок дар конфронс омадам	Man ba injo baroi ishtirok dar konfrons omadam
I'm in Tajikistan for tourism	Ман ба инҷо ҳамчун турист омадам	Man ba injo hamchun turist omadam
I'm from America	Ман аз Америка мебошам	Man az Amerika mebosham
I'm from England	Ман аз Инглистон мебошам	Man az Ingliston mebosham
I'm from Australia	Ман аз Австралия мебошам	Man az Avstraliya mebosham
Where are you from?	Шумо аз куҷо ҳастед?	Shumo az kujo hasted?
What do you do?	Шумо чӣ кор мекунед?	Shumo chi kor mekuned?
I'm a businessman	Ман соҳибкор ҳастам	Man sohibkor hastam
I'm a student	Ман донишҷӯ ҳастам	Man donishju hastam
I'm an engineer	Ман муҳандис мебошам	Man muhandis mebosham
I'm a lawyer	Ман ҳуқуқшинос ҳастам	Man huquqshinos hastam
I'm a doctor	Ман духтур ҳастам	Man duhtur hastam
Are you married?	Шумо оиладор ҳастед?	Shumo oilador hasted?
I'm married	Ман оиладор мебошам	Man oilador mebosham
This is my wife	Ин ҳамсари ман аст	In hamsari man ast
This is my husband.	Ин шавҳари ман аст	In shavhari man ast

I have one child	Ман як фарзанд дорам	Man yak farzand doram
I have two children	Ман ду фарзанд дорам	Man du farzand doram
I have three children	Ман се фарзанд дорам	Man se farzand doram
I have four children	Ман чор фарзанд дорам	Man cor farzand doram
I have five children	Ман панҷ фарзанд дорам	Man panç farzand doram
How old is your son?	Писари шумо чандсола ҳаст?	Pisari shumo chandsola hast?
How old is your daughter?	Духтари шумо чандсола ҳаст?	Duhtari shumo chandsola hast?
How many children do you have?	Шумо чанд фарзанд доред?	Shumo chand farzand dored?
Thank you	Ташаккур.	Tashakkur.
Here is my email	Марҳамат, почтаи электронии ман	Marhamat, poctai elektronii man
Do you use Facebook?	Шумо аз Facebook истифода мебаред?	Shumo az Facebook istifoda mebared?
Excuse me	Бубахшед	Bubahshed
Goodbye	Хайр	Hayr
Have a good night	Шаби хӯш	Shabi khush

b. Opinions/States of Being	b. Фикру ақида/Ҳолатҳо	b Fikru aqida/Holatho
GENERAL	УМУМӢ	UMUMI
I am hot	Ман гарм шудам	Man garm shudam
I am cold	Ман хунук хӯрда истодаам	Man khunuk hurda istodaam
I am tired	Ман монда шудам	Man monda shudam
I am sleepy	Ман хоб дорам	Man khob doram
I am jetlagged	Ман хеле монда шудам (бо сабаби парвози тӯлонӣ)	Man khele monda shudam (bo sababi parvozi tuloni)
I am hungry	Ман гурусна ҳастам	Man gurusna hastam
I am thirsty	Ман ташна ҳастам	Man tashna hastam

I need to use the restroom	Ман ба ҳоҷтхона эҳтиёҷ дорам	Man ba hojthona ehtiyoj doram
I need to smoke.	Ман бояд тамоку кашам	Man boyad tamoku kasham
Did you enjoy that?	Ба шумо маъқул шуд?	Ba shumo ma'qul shud?
I thought it was ...	Ман фикр кардам, ки он...	Man fikr kardam, ki on...
... amazing	...ҳайратангез буд	...hayratangez bud
... beautiful.	...зебо буд.	...zebo bud.
... okay	...хуб буд	...huв bud
... interesting	...аҷиб буд	...ajib bud
... unusual	...ғайриоддӣ буд	...ghayriodi bud
... dull	...дилгир буд	...dilgir bud
... overly expensive	...хеле гарон буд	...hele garon bud

c. Inviting People Out (Music/Nightclubs/ Performing Arts)	**с. Одамонро (ба Мусиқӣ/Клубҳо/ Маҳфилҳо) даъват кардан**	**c. Odamonro (ba Musiki/Klubho/ Mahfilho) da'vat kardan**
Would you like to go out tonight?	Шумо имшаб ба тамошо меравед?	Shumo imshab ba tamosho meraved?
What kind of things could we do at night?	Чӣ чизҳоро мо метавонем, ки шаб анҷом диҳем?	Chi chizhoro mo metavonem, ki shab anjom dihem?
Are you free ...	Шумо машғул нестед	Shumo mashghul nested
... tonight?	... имшаб?	... imshab?
... tomorrow?	... пагоҳ?	... pagoh?
... this weekend?	... охири ин ҳафта?	... ohiri in hafta?
When are you free?	Шумо кай машғул нестед?	Shumo kay mashghul nested?
Would you like to come with me?	Шумо мехоҳед, ки бо ман биёед?	Shumo mehohed, ki bo man biyoed?
Yes of course.	Албатта.	Albatta.
I'm sorry, I can't.	Мутаассифам, ман наметавонам.	Mutaassifam, man nametavonam.

Would you like to go ...	Оё Шумо мехоҳед, ки ба ... равед?	Oyo shumo mehohed, ki ba ... raved?
... to a bar?	... ба бар?	... ba bar?
... to a café?	... ба қаҳвахона?	... ba qahvahona?
... to a lounge?	... ба истироҳатгоҳ?	... ba istirohatgoh?
... to a concert?	... ба консерт?	... ba konsert?
... to a restaurant?	... ба тарабхона?	... ba tarabhona?
... to the movies?	... ба кино?	... ba kino?
... to a party?	... ба шабнишинӣ?	... ba shabnishini?
What time should we meet?	Соати чанд мо бояд воҳӯрем?	Soati chand mo boyad vohurem?
Where should we meet?	Мо бояд дар куҷо воҳӯрем?	Mo boyad dar kujo vohurem?
Will you pick me up?	Шумо омада маро мегиред?	Shumo omada maro megired?
I will pick you up.	Ман омада шуморо мегирам.	Man omada shumoro megiram.
What kind of music do you like?	Чӣ навъи мусиқӣ ба шумо писанд меояд?	Chi nav'i musiqi ba shumo pisand meoyad.
I like ...	Ба ман... маъқул аст	Ba man... ma'qul ast
... pop.	... поп	... pop
... rock.	... рок	... rok
... hip hop.	... ҳип ҳоп	... hip hop
... country.	... кантрӣ	... kantri.
... R&B.	... R&B.	... R&B.
Who is your favorite singer?	Овозхони дӯстдоштаи шумо кист?	Ovozhoni dustdoshtai shumo kist?
My favorite singer is ...	Овозхони дӯстдоштаи ман...	Ovozhoni dustdoshtai man...
Do you like ...	Оё шумо...-ро дӯст медоред?	Oyo shumo...-ro dust medored?
... to dance?	... рақс кардан?	... raqs kardan?
... to go to concerts?	... ба консерт рафтан?	... ba konsert raftan?
... to go to the theater?	... ба театр рафтан?	... ba teatr raftan?
... to go to the opera?	... ба опера рафтан?	... ba opera raftan?

... to go to the symphony?	... ба симфония рафтан?	... ba simfoniya raftan?
I do like ...	Ба ман ... маъкул аст	Ba man ... ma'qul ast
I don't like ...	Ба ман ... маъкул нест	Ba man ... ma'qul nest
I want to ...	Ман мехохам, ки ...	Man mehoham, ki ...
... go to a concert.	... ба консерт равам.	... ba konsert ravam.
... go to the theater.	... ба театр равам.	... ba teatr ravam.
... go to the symphony.	... ба симфония равам.	... ba simfoniya ravam.
... go to the opera.	... ба опера равам.	... ba opera ravam.
Do you want to ...	Оё Шумо мехохед, ки ...	Oyo shumo mehohed, ki ...
... go to a concert?	... ба консерт равед?	... ba konsert raved?
... go to the theater?	... ба театр равед?	... ba teatr raved?
... go to the symphony?	... ба симфония равед?	... ba simfoniya raved?
... go to the opera?	... ба опера равед?	... ba opera raved?
Could we buy tickets?	Оё мо метавонем, ки чипта харидорй намоем?	Oyo mo metavonem, ki chipta kharidori namoem?
How much are the tickets?	Чипиахо чанд пул хастанд?	Chipiaho chand pul hastand?
I want the cheapest tickets please.	Лутфан, ба ман чиптахои арзонтаринро дихед.	Lutfan, ba man chiptahoi arzontarinro dihed.
I want the best tickets please.	Лутфан, ба ман чиптахои бехтаринро дихед.	Lutfan, ba man chiptahoi behtarinro dihed.
Where is the concert?	Консерт дар кучо аст?	Konsert dar kujo ast?
I need to buy ...	Ман бояд ... харидорй намоям	Man boyad ... kharidori namoyam
... one ticket, please.	... лутфан, як чипта.	... lutfan, yak chipta.
... two tickets, please.	... лутфан, ду чипта.	...lutfan, du chipta.
That was great.	Олй буд.	Oli bud.
That was long.	Дароз буд.	Daroz bud.
That was amazing.	Хайратангез буд.	Hayratangez bud.
That was okay.	Хуб буд.	Hub bud.

What kind of movies do you like?	Чй навъи кино ба шумо писанд меояд.	Chi nav'i kino ba shumo pisand meoyad.
I like ...	Ба ман... маъқул аст	Ba man... ma'qul ast
... action.	... ҷанг.	... jang.
... animated films.	... санъати тасвирй	... san'ati tasviri.
... drama.	... драма	... drama
... documentaries.	... филмҳои мустанад	... filmhoi mustanad
... comedy.	... мазҳакавй	... mazhakavi
... thrillers.	... триллер	... triller
... science fiction.	... илми тахаюлй	... ilmi tahayuli
... horror.	... тарсовар	... tarsovar
... romantic comedy.	... мазҳакавй романтикй	... mazhakavi romantiki
Could we go to the movies tonight?	Имшаб ба кино меравем?	Imshab ba kino meravem?
When can we go to the movies?	Кай ба кино меравем?	Kay ba kino meravem?
What movies are playing?	Кадом кино аст?	Kadom kino ast?
How much are the tickets?	Чиптаҳо чанд пул ҳастанд?	Chiptaho chand pul hastand?
Is the theater far from here?	Театр аз инҷо дур аст?:	Teatr az injo dur ast?

d. Hiking	**d. Роҳ гашта сайр кардан**	**d. Roh gashta sayr kardan**
Do you like to hike?	Шумо роҳ гашта сайр карданро дӯст медоред?	Shumo roh gashta sayr kardan dust medored?
I love to hike.	Ман роҳ гашта сайр карданро дӯст медорам.	Man roҳ gashta sayr kardan dust medoram.
What is the weather going to be like?	Обу ҳаво чй хел мешуда бошад?	Obu havo chi khel meshuda boshad?
It will be ...	Обу ҳаво...	Obu havo...
... cold.	... хунук мешавад.	... khunuk meshavad.
... cloudy.	... абрнок мешавад.	... abrnok meshavad.
... snowing.	... барф меборад.	... barf meborad.

... sunny.	... офтоб**й** мешав**ад**.	... oftob**i** meshav**ad**.
... warm.	... гарм мешав**ад**.	... garm meshav**ad**.
... hot.	... гарм мешав**ад**.	... garm meshav**ad**.
When can we go?	Мо к**ай** мерав**ем**?	Mo k**ay** merav**em**?
Is it safe?	О**ё** бехат**ар** аст?	O**yo** behat**ar** ast?
Do we need to buy water?	О**ё** бар**ои** харидор**й** намудан**и** об ни**ёз** дор**ем**?	O**yo** bar**oi** kharidor**i** namudan**i** ob ni**yoz** dor**em**?
Is the water safe to drink?	О**ё** н**ӯ**шидан аз об бехат**ар** аст?	O**yo** nushid**an** az ob bekhat**ar** ast?
Do we need to buy food?	О**ё** бар**ои** харидор**й** намудан**и** х**ӯ**роквор**й** ни**ёз** дор**ем**?	O**yo** bar**oi** kharidor**i** namudan**i** hurokvor**i** ni**yoz** dor**em**?
Will we need a guide?	О**ё** ба мо роҳбал**ад** лоз**им** мешав**ад**?	O**yo** ba mo rohbal**ad** loz**im** meshav**ad**?
Is it scenic there?	Манзарад**ор** аст?	Manzarad**or** ast?
How long is the hike?	Сайр ч**й** қад**ар** т**ӯл** мекаш**ад**?	Sayr chi qadar tul mekash**ad**?
How long is the drive?	Бо мош**ин** ч**й** қад**ар** т**ӯл** мекаш**ад**?	Bo moshin chi qadar tul mekash**ad**?
How long is the climb?	Баромад**ан** ч**й** қад**ар** т**ӯл** мекаш**ад**?	Baromad**an** chi qadar tul mekash**ad**?
I'm looking for ...	М**ан** ... ҷустуҷ**ӯ** дор**ам**	Man ... justuj**u** dor**am**
... the campsite	... ҷ**ой** бар**ои** к**е**мпинг	... j**oy** bar**oi** k**e**mping
... the toilet	... ҳоҷатх**она**	... hojath**ona**
What time does the sun go down?	Ғур**у**би офт**об** со**ати** чанд аст?	Ghur**u**bi oft**ob** so**ati** chand ast?

e. Sports   е. Варзиш   e. Varzish

What sport do you love?	Кад**ом** нам**уди** варз**иш** ба шум**о** пис**анд** аст?	Kad**om** namudi varzish ba shum**o** pis**and** ast?
I love ...	М**ан** ... -ро д**ӯ**ст мед**орам**	Man ... -ro dust med**oram**
... football	... футб**ол**	... futb**ol**
... hockey	... хокк**ей**	... hokk**ey**
... basketball	... баскетб**ол**	... basketb**ol**
... baseball	... бейсб**ол**	... beysb**ol**

26

... soccer	... футбол	... futbol
... boxing	... бокс	... boks
Do you play ...	Шумо... бозӣ мекунед?	Shumo... bozi mekuned?
... football?	... футбол	... futbol
... hockey?	... хоккей	... hokkey
... basketball?	... баскетбол	... basketbol
... baseball?	... бейсбол	... beysbol
... soccer?	... футбол	... futbol
... volleyball?	... волейбол	... voleybol
Yes, I do.	Бале.	Bale.
A little bit.	Каме.	Kame.
No, not much.	Не, на он қадар.	Ne, na on qadar.
Do you ...	Оё шумо...	Oyo shumo...
... go running?	... медавед?	... medaved?
... go to the gym?	... ба варзишгоҳ меравед?	... ba varzishgoh meraved?
Could we play?	Бозӣ мекунем?	bozi mekunem?
I'd like to play.	Ман мехоҳам, ки бозӣ кунам.	Man mekhoham, ki bozi kunam.
I'm sorry, I can't play.	Мутаассифам, ман бозӣ карда наметавонам.	Mutaassifam, man bozi karda nametavonam.
I'm tired.	Ман монда шудам	Man monda shudam
I think I need a break.	Фикр мекунам, ки ман бояд истироҳат намоям.	Fikr mekunam, ki man boyad istirohat namoyam.
Can we go to a game?	Ба ягон бозӣ меравем?	Ba yagon bozi meravem?
Where is it located?	Дар куҷо воқеъ аст?	Dar kujo voq'e ast?
Who's playing?	Кӣ бозӣ дорад?	Ki bozi dorad?
How much are the tickets?	Чиптаҳо чанд пул ҳастанд?	Chiptaho chand pul hastand?
I need ...	Ба ман ... лозим аст	Ba man ... lozim ast
... one ticket, please.	... лутфан, як чипта.	... lutfan, yak chipta.
... two tickets, please.	... лутфан, ду чипта.	... lutfan, du chipta.
That was great!	Олӣ буд.	Oli bud.

He's an awesome player!	Ӯ як бозингари **оли** аст!	U yak bozingari **oli** ast!
That was long!	Дароз буд.	Dar**oz** bud.

f. Sex & Romance | f. Алоқаи чинсӣ ва Хаёлпарастӣ | f. Alokai jinsi va Heyolparasti

CONVERSATION STARTERS	ОҒОЗИ СУҲБАТ	OGH**OZ**I SUHB**A**T
Hey, you look like you're having the most fun out of anybody here.	Ба назар мерасад, ки шумо дар инҷо вақти хӯш гузаронида истодаед.	Ba nazar merasad, ki shumo dar injo vaqti khush guzaronida istodaed.
Hi, are you from around here?	Салом, шумо дар наздикӣ зиндагӣ мекунед?	Salom, shumo dar nazdiki zindagi mekuned?
Can I buy you a drink?	Барои шумо нӯшокӣ харидорӣ намоям?	Baroi shumo nushoki kharidorinamoyam?
Want to dance?	Рақс кардан мехоҳед?	Raqs kardan mekhohed?
I'm having a great time with you.	Бо шумо вақтам хӯш аст.	Bo shumo vaqtam khush ast.
You're awesome.	Шумо олӣ ҳастед	Shumo oli hasted
I'm having the time of my life.	Ман беҳтарин лаҳзаҳои ҳаётамро гузаронида истодаам.	Man behtarin lahzahoi hayotamro guzaronida istodaam.
Want to go some place quiet?	Ба ягон ҷои оромтар рафтан мехоҳед?	Ba yagon joi oromtar raftan mekhohed?
Want to go outside with me?	Ба берун меравем?	Ba berun meravem?
You're beautiful.	Шумо зебо ҳастед	Shumo zebo hasted
Let's go inside.	Биё, ба дарун равем.	Biyo, ba darun ravem.
SEX	Ҷинс	Jins
Kiss me.	Ба ман бибӯсам	Ba man bibusam
Touch me here.	Маро ба инҷо нарасад	Maro ba injo narasad
Take this off.	Дур либос шумо.	Dur libos shumo.
Does that feel good?	Оё ин хуб?	Oyo in khub?

28

You like that.	Оё шумо мехоҳед	Oyo shumo mekhohed
Let's use a condom.	Биёед истифода рифола.	Biyoed istifoda rifola.
I can only do it with a condom.	Ман танҳо метавонад ин корро бо рифола.	Man tanho metavonad in korro bo rifola.
Stop!	Бас!	Bas!
Don't do that.	Оё он кор!	Oyo on kor!
I like when you do that.	Ман мехоҳам, ки шумо ин корро!	Man mekhoham , ki shumo in korro!
Keep going.	Давом диҳем.	Davom dihem.
That feels so good.	Ки ҳис хуб.	Ki his khub.
That was incredible.	Олиҷаноб.	Olijanob.
Let's do it again.	Биёед ба он боз.	Biyoed ba on boz.
I want you.	Ман туро мехоҳам.	Man turo mekhoham.
I love your body.	Ман дӯст ҷисми худ.	Man dust jismi khud.
You're beautiful	Шумо зебо ҳастед.	Shumo zebo hasted.
I love you.	Ман туро дӯст медорам.	Man turo dust medoram.
I want to see you again.	Бо ту боз вохӯрдан мехоҳам.	Bo tu boz vokhurdan mekhoham.
Would you like to meet me tomorrow?	Фардо вомехӯрем?	Fardo vomekhurem?
Would you like to meet me on the weekend?	Охири ҳафта вомехӯрем?	Okhiri hafta vomekhurem?
Would you like to give me your phone number?	Ба ман рақами телефонатро медиҳӣ?	Ba man raqami telefonatro medihi?
Would you like to give me your email?	Ба ман почтаи электрониатро медиҳӣ?	Ba man pochtai elektroniatro medihi?

3. EMERGENCIES

General

3. ҲОЛАТҲОИ ФАВҚУЛОДДА

Умумӣ

3. HOLATHOI FAVQULODDA

Umumi

English	Tajik (Cyrillic)	Tajik (Latin)
Is it safe?	Оё бехатар аст?	Oyo bekhatar ast?
This is an emergency!	Ин ҳолати фавқулодда аст!	In holati favqulodda ast!
Help!	Ёрӣ диҳед!	Yori dihed!
Be careful!	Эҳтиёт бош!	Ehtiyot bosh!
Stop!	Bas!	Bas!
Call the ambulance!	Ба ёрии таъҷилӣ занг зан!	Bo yorii ta'jili zang zan!
Call the police!	Ба пулис занг зан!	Ba pulis zang zan!
He is hurt.	Ба ӯ зарар расидааст.	Ba u zarar rasidaast.
She is hurt.	Ба ӯ зарар расидааст.	Ba u zarar rasidaast.
There has been an accident.	Дар онҷо садама буд.	Dar onjo sadama bud.
Can I use your phone?	Аз телефони мобилии Шумо истифода бурда метавонам?	Az telefoni mobilii shumo istifoda burda metavonam?
Could you help me please?	Лутфан, ба ман ёрӣ диҳед?	Lutfan, ba man yori dihed?
I have been robbed.	Маро ғорат карданд.	Maro ghorat kardand.
I have been assaulted.	Ба ман ҳамла карданд.	Ba man hamla kardand.
She has been raped.	Ба номуси ӯ таҷовуз карданд.	Ba nomusi u tajovuz kardand.
He has been assaulted.	Ба ӯ ҳамла карданд.	Ba u hamla kardand.
I lost my ...	Ман... -ро гум кардам	Man... -ro gum kardam
... passport	... шиносномам	... shinosnomam
... money	... пулам	... pulam
... wallet	... ҷувздонам	... juvzdonam
It was a man.	Ӯ мард буд.	U mard bud.
It was a woman	Ӯ зан буд.	U zan bud.
It was him.	Ӯ буд.	U bud.
It was her.	Ӯ буд.	U bud.

30

I need a lawyer	Ба ман ҳуқуқшинос дозим аст.	Ba man huquqshinos lozim ast.
I need to contact the American embassy.	Ман бояд бо сафоратхонаи Америка дар тамос шавам.	Man boyad bo saforatkhonai Amerika dar tamos shavam.
I need to contact the British embassy.	Ман бояд бо сафоратхонаи Бритонё дар тамос шавам.	Man boyad bo saforatkhonai Britonyo dar tamos shavam

4. MEDICAL CARE   4. КӮМАКИ ТИББӢ   4. KUMAKI TIBBI

I need to go to the hospital.	Ман бояд ба беморхона равам.	Man boyad ba bemorkhona ravam.
Where is the hospital?	Беморхона дар куҷо аст?	Bemorkhona dar kujo ast?
Where is the pharmacy?	Дорухона дар куҷо аст?	Dorukhona dar kujo ast?
I lost my medication.	Ман доруямро гум кардам.	Man doruyamro gum kardam.
I need this medication.	Ба ман ин дору лозим аст.	Ba man in doru lozim ast.
I'm on medication for ...	Ман аз ин дору барои... истифода мебарам.	Man az in doru baroi... istifoda mebaram.
I need new glasses.	Ба ман айнакҳои нав лозим аст.	Ba man aynakhoi nav lozim ast.
I need new contact lenses.	Ба ман линзаҳои нав лозим аст.	Ba man linzaҳoi nav lozim ast.
I need the receipt, please.	Ба ман расид лозим аст.	Ba man rasid lozim ast.
I'm hurt.	Ба ман зарар расидааст.	Ba man zarar rasidaast.
He is hurt.	Ба ӯ зарар расидааст.	Ba ū zarar rasidaast.
She is hurt.	Ба ӯ зарар расидааст.	Ba ū zarar rasidaast.
I'm sick	Ман беморам.	Man bemoram.
He is sick.	Ӯ бемор аст.	Ū bemor ast.
She is sick.	Ӯ бемор аст	Ū bemor ast

It hurts right here ...	Инҷо дард мекунад...	Injo dard mekunad...
I can't move my ...	Ман... ҳаракат карда наметавонам.	Man... harakat karda nametavonam.
I'm allergic to something.	Ман ба чизе ҳассосият дорам.	Man ba chize hasosiyat doram.
I was throwing up.	Ман партофта истода будам.	Man partofta istoda budam.
He was throwing up.	Ӯ партофта истода буд.	Ū partofta istoda bud.
She was throwing up.	Ӯ партофта истода буд.	Ū partofta istoda bud.
I have chills.	Ман табларза дорам.	Man tablarza doram.
I feel weak.	Ман заиф ҳастам.	Man zaif hastam.
I feel dizzy.	Сарам чарх мезанад.	Saram charkh mezanad.
I can't sleep.	Ман хоб карда наметвонам.	Man khob karda nametvonam.
I have a headache.	Сарам дард мекунад.	Saram dard mekunad.
I need antibiotics.	Ба ман антибиотик лозим аст.	Ba man antibiotik lozim ast.
How many times a day should I take this?	Дар як рӯз чанд маротиба инро истифода барам?	Dar yak ruz chand marotiba inro istifoda baram?
He is having ...	Ӯ...	U...
... an epileptic fit.	... касалии эпилептикӣ дорад.	... kasalii epileptiki dorad.
... an asthma attack.	... зиққи нафас (астма) дорад.	... ziqqi nafas (astma) dorad.
... a heart attack.	... сактаи дил дорад.	... saktai dil dorad.
I have a fever ...	Ман таб дорам...	Man tab doram...
She has a fever ...	Ӯ таб дорад...	U tab dorad...
He has a fever ...	Ӯ таб дорад...	U tab dorad...

Women	**Занҳо**	**Zanho**
I'm on the pill.	Ман дору истеъмол мекунам.	Man doru istemol mekunam.

I need the morning after pill.	Ба ман ҳаби котрасептивӣ лозим аст.	Ba man habi kotraseptivi lozim ast.
I need a pregnancy test.	Ба ман тест барои муайян намудани ҳомиладорӣ лозим аст.	Ba man test baroi muayyan namudani homiladori lozim ast.
I have missed my period.	Ман ҳайз нашудам.	Man hayz nashudam.
I might be pregnant.	Шояд, ки ман ҳомиладор бошам.	Shoyad, ki man homilador bosham.
I'm pregnant.	Ман ҳомиладорам.	Man homiladoram.
I have a yeast infection.	Ман касалии сирояткунанда (дрожжевая инфекция) дорам.	Man kasalii siroyatkunanda (drozhzhevaya infektsiya) doram.
I have a UTI (urinary tract infection).	Ман сирояти рӯдаи пешоб дорам.	Man siroyati rudai peshob doram.

5. MINI DICTIONARY	5. ФАРҲАНГИ ХУРД	5. FARHANGI KHURD
a. English to Tajik	a. Англисӣ-Тоҷикӣ	a. Anglisi-Tojiki

English	Tajik	Pronunciation

A

English	Tajik	Pronunciation
Aboard	Дар дохили	Dar dokhili
About	Тақрибан	Taqriban
Above	Дар болои	Dar boloi
Accident	Ҳодиса	Hodisa
Account	Ҳисоб	Hisob
Across	Аз байни	Az bayni
Adapter	Созгор	Sozgor
Address	Суроға	Surogha
Admit	Қабул кардан	Qabul kardan
Adult	Болиғ,	Boligh
Advice	Тавсия	Tavsiya
Afraid	Тарсидан	Tarsidan
After	Баъд аз	Ba'd az
Age	Синну сол	Sinnu sol
Ago	Пеш	Pesh
Agree	Розӣ шудан	Rozi shudan
Ahead	Ба пеш	Ba pesh
Air	Ҳаво	Havo
Air conditioning	Кондитсионер	Konditsioner
Airline	Хати ҳавой	Khati havoi
Airplane	Тайёра	Tayyora
Airport	Фурудгоҳ	Furudgoh
Aisle	Ҷои гузар	Joi guzar
Alarm clock	Соати зангдор	Soati zangdor
Alcohol	Нушокии спиртй	Nushokii spirti
All	Ҳама	Hama
Allergy	Аллергия	Allergiya
Alone	Танҳо	Tanho

English	Tajik	Pronunciation
Already	Аллакай	Allakay
Also	Ҳам	Ham
Always	Ҳамеша	Hamesha
Ancient	Куҳна	Kuhna
And	Ва	Va
Angry	Хашмгин	Khashmgin
Animal	Ҳайвон	Hayvon
Ankle	Буҷули пой	Bujuli poy
Another	Дигар	Digar
Answer	Ҷавоб	Javob
Antique	Қадима	Qadima
Apartment	Хона	Khona
Apple	Себ	Seb
Appointment	Вохӯрй	Vokhuri
Argue	Баҳс кардан	Bahs kardan
Arm	Даст	Dast
Arrest	Ҳабс кардан	Ҳabs kardan
Arrivals	Расиданҳо	Rasidanҳo
Arrive	Расидан	Rasidan
Art	Санъат	San"at
Artist	Ҳунарманд	Ҳunarmand
Ask (questinoning)	Савол додан	Savol dodan
Ask (request)	Хоҳиш кардан	Khoҳish kardan
Aspirin	Аспирин	Aspirin
At	Дар	Dar
ATM	Банкомат	Bankomat
Awful	Даҳшатангез	Dahshatangez

B

Baby	Кӯдак	Kudak
Babysitter	Доя	Doya
Back (body)	Пушт	Pusht
Back (backward position)	Пас	Pas
Backpack	Борхалта	Borkhalta

English	Tajik	Pronunciation
Bacon	Бекон	Bekon
Bad	Бад	Bad
Bag	Сумка	Sumka
Baggage	Бағоҷ	Baghoj
Baggage claim	Гирифтани бағоҷ	Giriftani baghoj
Bakery	Нонпазхона	Nonpazkhona
Ball (sports)	Тӯб	Tub
Banana	Банан	Banan
Band (musician)	Гурӯҳ	Guruh
Bandage	Захмбанд	Zakhmband
Band-Aid	Захмбанди часпак (лейкопластырь)	Zakhmbandi chaspak (leykoplastyr')
Bank	Бонк	Bonk
Bank account	Ҳисоби бонкӣ	Hisobi bonki
Basket	Сабад	Sabad
Bath	Ҳамом	Hamom
Bathing suit	Костюм барои оббозй	Kostyum baroi obbozi
Bathroom	Ҳамом	Hamom
Battery	Батарея	Batareya
Be	Будан	Budan
Beach	Соҳил	Sohil
Beautiful	Зебо	Zebo
Because	Барои он	Baroi on
Bed	Кат	Kat
Bedroom	Ҷои хоб	Joi khob
Beef	Гушти гов	Gushti gov
Beer	Оби ҷав	Obi jav
Before	Қабл аз	Qabl az
Behind	Пас	Pas
Below	Дар поён	Dar poyon
Beside	Дар бари	Dar bari
Best	Беҳтарин	Behtarin
Bet	Шарт бастан	Shart bastan
Between	Дар байни	Dar bayni
Bicycle	Велосипед	Velosiped

English	Tajik	Pronunciation
Big	Калон	Kalon
Bike	Велосипед	Velosiped
Bill (bill of sale)	Расид	Rasid
Bird	Парранда	Parranda
Birthday	Зодрӯз	Zodruz
Bite (dog bite)	Газидан	Gazidan
Bitter	Талх	Talkh
Black	Сиёҳ	Siyoh
Blanket	Курпа	Kurpa
Blind	Кур	Kur
Blood	Хун	Khun
Blue (dark blue)	Кабуди серранг	Kabudi serrang
Blue (light blue)	Кабуди беранг	Kabudi berang
Board (climb aboard)	Савор шудан	Savor shudan
Boarding pass	Талони саворшавӣ	Taloni savorshavi
Boat	Киштӣ	Kishti
Body	Бадан	Badan
Book	Китоб	Kitob
Bookshop	Мағозаи китоб	Maghozai kitob
Boots (shoes)	Мӯза	Muza
Border	Сарҳад	Sarhad
Bored	Дилгир	Dilgir
Boring	Дилгиркунанда	Dilgirkunanda
Borrow	Қарз гирифтан	Qarz giriftan
Both	Ҳарду	Hardu
Bottle	Шиша	Shisha
Bottle opener (beer)	Кушояндаи шиша	Kushoyandai shisha
Bottle opener (corkscrew)	Кушояндаи шиша	Kushoyandai shisha
Bottom (butt)	Сурин	Surin
Bottom (on bottom)	Поин	Poin
Bowl	Коса	Kosa
Box	Қуттӣ	Qutti
Boy	Писарбача	Pisarbacha
Boyfriend	Маъшуқ	Ma'shuq
Bra	Синабанд	Sinaband

English	Tajik	Pronunciation
Brave	Ҷасур	Jasur
Bread	Нон	Non
Break	Танаффус	Tanaffus
Breakfast	Хӯроки саҳар	Khuroki sahar
Breathe	Нафас кашидан	Nafas kashidan
Bribe	Пора	Pora
Bridge	Пул	Pul
Bring	Овардан	Ovardan
Broken (breaking)	Шикастагӣ	Shikastagi
Brother	Бародар	Barodar
Brown	Қаҳваранг	Qahvarang
Brush	Мисвок	Misvok
Bucket	Сатил	Satil
Bug	Кана	Kana
Build	Сохтан	Sokhtan
Builder	Сохтмончӣ	Sokhtmonchi
Building	Бино	Bino
Burn	Сухтан	Sukhtan
Bus	Автобус	Avtobus
Bus station	Истгоҳи автобусҳо	Istgohi avtobusho
Bus stop	Истгоҳи автобусҳо	Istgohi avtobusho
Business	Фаъолият	Fa'oliyat,
Busy	Машғул	Mashghul
But	Лекин	Lekin
Butter	Равған	Ravghan
Butterfly	Шапалак	Shapalak
Buy	Харидан	Kharidan

C

Cake (wedding cake)	Торт	Tort
Cake (birthday cake)	Торт	Tort
Call	Фарёд кардан	Faryod kardan
Call (telephone call)	Занг задан	Zang zadan
Camera	Камера	Kamera
Camp	Лагер	Lager

English	Tajik	Pronunciation
Campfire	Гулхан	Gulkhan
Campsite	Кемпинг	Kemping
Can (have the ability)	Тавонистан	Tavonistan
Can (allowed)	Тавонистан	Tavonistan
Can (aluminium can)	Қуттӣ	Qutti
Cancel	Бекор кардан	Bekor kardan
Candle	Шамъ	Sham'
Candy	Қанд	Qand
Car	Мошин	Moshin
Cards (playing cards)	Кортхо	Kortho
Care for	Нигоҳубин кардан	Nigohubin kardan
Carpenter	Дуредгар	Duredgar
Carriage	Фойтун	Foytun
Carrot	Сабзӣ	Sabzi
Carry	Расондан	Rasondan
Cash	Нақд	Naqd
Cash (deposit a check)	Нақд	Naqd
Cashier	Хазиначӣ	Hazinachi
Castle	Қалъа	Qal'a
Cat	Гурба	Gurba
Cathedral	Калисои ҷомеъ	Kalisoi jome
Celebration	Ҷашн	Jashn
Cell phone	Телефони мобилӣ	Telefoni mobili
Cemetery	Қабристон	Qabriston
Cent	Сент	Sent
Centimeter	Сантиметр	Santimetr
Center	Марказ	Markaz
Cereal	Ғалладона	Ghalladona
Chair	Курсӣ	Kursi
Chance	Шонс	Shons
Change	Тағйирот	Taghyirot
Change (coinage)	Майда	Mayda
Change (pocket change)	Майда	Mayda
Changin room	Ҳуҷраи либос ивазкунӣ	Hujrai libos ivazkuni

English	Tajik	Pronunciation
Chat up	Гуфтугӯ кардан	Guftugu kardan
Cheap	Арзон	Arzon
Cheat	Фиреб кардан	Fireb kardan
Cheese	Панир	Panir
Chef	Сарошпаз	Saroshpaz
Cherry	Гелос	Gelos
Chest (torso)	Қафаси сина	Qafasi sina
Chicken	Чӯҷа	Chuja
Child	Кӯдак	Kudak
Children	Кӯдакон	Kudakon
Chocolate	Шоколад	Shokolad
Choose	Интихоб кардан	Intihob kardan
Christmas	Мавлуди Исо	Mavludi Iso
Cider	Шароби себ	Sharobi seb
Cigar	Сигар	Sigar
Cigarette	Сигарет	Sigaret
City	Шаҳр	Shahr
City center	Маркази шаҳр	Markazi shahr
Class (categorize)	Синф	Sinf
Clean	Тоза	Toza
Cleaning	Тозакунӣ	Tozakuni
Climb	Баромадан	Baromadan
Clock	Соат	Soat
Close	Пӯшидан	Pushidan
Close (closer)	Наздик	Nazdik
Closed	Пӯшида	Pushida
Clothing	Либос	Libos
Clothing store	Мағозаи либос	Maghozai libos
Cloud	Абр	Abr
Cloudy	Абрнок	Abrnok
Coast	Соҳил	Sohil
Coat	Палто	Palto
Cockroach	Нонхӯрак	Honhurak
Cocktail	Коктейл	Kokteil
Cocoa	Какао	Kakao
Coffee	Қаҳва	Qahva

40

English	Tajik	Pronunciation
Coins	Тангаҳо	Tangaho
Cold	Хунук	Hunuk
College	Коллеҷ	Kollej
Color	Ранг	Rang
Comb	Шона	Shona
Come	Омадан	Omadan
Comfortable	Вароҳат	Barohat
Compass	Компас	Kompas
Complain	Шикоят кардан	Shikoyat kardan
Complimentary (on the house)	Ройгон	Roygon
Computer	Компютер	Kompyuter
Concert	Консерт	Konsert
Conditioner (conditioning treatment)	Кондитсионер	Konditsioner
Contact lens solution	Маҳлули линзаҳо	Mahluli linzaho
Contact lenses	Линзаҳо	Linzaho
Contract	Шартнома	Shartnoma
Cook	Пухтан	Puhtan
Cookie	Кулчаҳои қандин	Kulchahoi qandin
Cool (mild temperature)	Салқин	Salqin
Corn	Ҷуворӣ	Juvori
Corner	Канор	Kanor
Cost	Арзидан	Arzidan
Cotton	Пахта	Pahta
Cotton balls	Тӯбчаҳои пахтагин	Tubchahoi pahtagin
Cough	Сулфидан	Sulfidan
Count	Ҳисоб кардан	Hisob kardan
Country	Кантрӣ	Kantri
Cow	Гов	Gov
Crafts	Ҳунар	Hunar
Crash	Садама	Sadama
Crazy	Девона	Devona
Cream (creamy)	Қаймоқ	Qaymoq

English	Tajik	Pronunciation
Cream (treatment)	Крем	Krem
Credit	Қарз	Qarz
Credit card	Корти кредитй	Korti krediti
Cross (crucifix)	Салиб	Salib
Crowded	Серодам	Serodam
Cruise	Шинокунй	Shinokuni
Custom	Урф	Urf
Customs	Гумрук	Gumruk
Cut	Буридан	Buridan
Cycle	Давра	Davra
Cycling	Велосипед рондан	Velosiped rondan
Cyclist	Велосипедист	Velosipedist

D

English	Tajik	Pronunciation
Dad	Падар	Padar
Daily	Ҳаррӯза	Harruza
Dance	Рақс кардан	Raqs kardan
Dancing	Рақс	Raqs
Dangerous	Хатарнок	Khatarnok
Dark	Торик	Torik
Date (important notice)	Сана	Sana
Date (specific day)	Сана	Sana
Date (companion)	Дӯст	Dust
Daughter	Духтар	Dukhtar
Dawn	Субҳ	Subh
Day	Рӯз	Ruz
Day after tomorrow	Рӯзи дигар	Ruzi digar
Day before yesterday	Рӯзи қабл аз дирӯз	Ruzi qabl az diruz
Dead	Мурда	Murda
Deaf	Кар	Kar
Deal (card dealer)	Тақсим кардан	Taqsim kardan
Decide	Қарор додан	Qaror dodan
Deep	Чуқур	Chuqur
Degrees (weather)	Дараҷа	Daraja

42

English	Tajik	Pronunciation
Delay	Дер кардан	Der kardan
Deliver	Расонидани	Rasonidani
Dentist	Дандонпизишк	Dandonpizishk
Deodorant	Дезодорант	Dezodorant
Depart	Тарк кардан	Tark kardan
Department store	Универмаг	Univermag
Departure	Тарк	Tark
Departure gate	Дарвоза	Darvoza
Deposit	Пасандоз	Pasandoz
Desert	Биёбон	Biyobon
Dessert	Ширинӣ	Shirini
Details	Тафсилот	Tafsilot
Diaper	Уребча	Urebcha
Diarrhea	Шикамрав	Shikamrav
Diary	Рӯзнома	Ruznoma
Die	Мурдан	Murdan
Diet	Парҳез	Parhez
Different	Мухталиф	Mukhtalif
Difficult	Душвор	Dushvor
Dinner	Таоми шом	Taomi shom
Direct	Рост	Rost
Direction	Самт	Samt
Dirty	Ифлос	Iflos
Disaster	Офат	Ofat
Disabled	Маъюб	Ma'yub
Dish	Коса	Kosa
Diving	Ғӯтазанӣ	Ghutazani
Dizzy	Чархзании сар	Charkhzanii sar
Do	Кардан	Kardan
Doctor	Духтур	Dukhtur
Dog	Саг	Sag
Door	Дар	Dar
Double	Дуто	Duto
Double bed	Кати дукаса	Kati dukasa
Double room	Ду ҳуҷрага	Du hujraga
Down	Поён	Poyon

English	Tajik	Pronunciation
Downhill	Фурориш	Furorish
Dream	Орзу	Orzu
Dress	Курта	Kurta
Drink (cocktail)	Нӯшидан	Nushidan
Drink (beverage)	Нӯшидан	Nushidan
Drink	Нӯшидан	Nushidan
Drive	Рондан	Rondan
Drums	Барабан	Baraban
Drunk	Маст	Mast
Dry	Хушк	Khushk
Dry (warm up)	Хушк кардан	Khushk kardan
Duck	Мурғобӣ	Murghobi

E

English	Tajik	Pronunciation
Each	Ҳар як	Har yak
Ear	Гуш	Gush
Early	Барвақт	Barvaqt
Earn	Касб кардан	Kasb kardan
East	Шарқ	Sharq
Easy	Осон	Oson
Eat	Хӯрдан	Khurdan
Education	Маориф	Maorif
Egg	Тухм	Tukhm
Electricity	Барқ	Barq
Elevator	Лифт	Lift
Embarrassed	Хиҷолат кашида	Khijolat kashida
Emergency	Ҳолатҳои фавқулодда	Holathoi favqulodda
Empty	Холӣ	Kholi
End	Охир	Okhir
English	Англисӣ	Anglisi
Enjoy (enjoying)	Баҳраманд шудан	Bahramand shudan
Enough	Кофӣ	Kofi
Enter	Даромадан	Daromadan
Entry	Ворид	Vorid

44

English	Tajik	Pronunciation
Escalator	Эскалатор	Eskalator
Euro	Евро	Yevro
Evening	Бегоҳ	Begoh
Every	Ҳар як	Har yak
Everyone	Ҳар як кас	Har yak kas
Everything	Ҳар як чиз	Har yak chiz
Exactly	Аниқ	Aniq
Exit	Баромад	Baromad
Expensive	Қимат	Qimat
Experience	Таҷриба	Tajriba
Eyes	Чашмҳо	Chashmho

F

Face	Рӯй	Ruy
Fall (autumnal)	Тирамоҳ	Tiramoh
Fall (falling)	Афтидан	Aftidan
Family	Оила	Oila
Famous	Машхур	Mashhur
Far	Дур	Dar
Fare	Роҳкиро	Rohkiro
Farm	Ферма	Ferma
Fast	Тез	Tez
Fat	Фарбеҳ	Farbeh
Feel (touching)	Ҳис кардан	His kardan
Feelings	Ҳиссиёт	Hissiyot
Female	Зан	Zan
Fever	Таб	Tab
Few	Якчанд	Yakchand
Fight	Ҷанг кардан	Jang kardan
Fill	Пур кардан	Pur kardan
Fine	Хуб	Khub
Finger	Ангушт	Angusht
Finish	Итмом	Itmom
Fire (heated)	Оташ	Otash
First	Якум	Yakum

English	Tajik	Pronunciation
First-aid kit	Доруқуттӣ	Doruqutti
Fish	Моҳӣ	Mohi
Flat	Хона	Khona
Floor (carpeting)	Фарш	Farsh
Floor (level)	Ошёна	Oshona
Flour	Орд	Ord
Flower	Гул	Gul
Fly	Парвоз кардан	Parvoz kardan
Foggy	Тумандор	Tumandor
Follow	Пайравӣ кардан	Payravi kardan
Food	Ғизо	Ghizo
Foot	Пой	Poy
Forest	Ҷангал	Jangal
Forever	Ҳамеша	Hamesha
Forget	Фаромуш кардан	Faromush kardan
Fork	Чангол	Changol
Foul	Қонуншиканӣ	Qonunshikani
Fragile	Зудшикан	Zudshikan
Free (at liberty)	Озод	Ozod
Free (no cost)	Ройгон	Roygon
Fresh	Тару тоза	Taru toza
Fridge	Яхдон	Yakhdon
Friend	Рафиқ	Rafik
From	Аз	Az
Frost	Сармо	Sarmo
Fruit	Мева	Meva
Fry	Бирён кардан	Biron kardan
Frying pan	Тезпазонак	Tezpazonak
Full	Пурра	Purra
Full-time	Вақти пурра	Vaqti purra
Fun	Хурсандӣ	Khursandi
Funny	Хандовар	Khandovar
Furniture	Мебел	Mebel
Future	Оянда	Oyanda

46

English	Tajik	Pronunciation

G

English	Tajik	Pronunciation
Game (match-up)	Бозй	Bozi
Game (event)	Бозй	Bozi
Garbage	Партов	Partov
Garbage can	Қуттии партовхо	Quttii partovho
Garden	Боғ	Bogh
Gas (gasoline)	Сӯзишворй	Suzishvori
Gate (airport)	Дарвоза	Darvoza
Gauze	Дока	Doka
Get	Гирифта	Girifta
Get off (disembark)	Фаромадан	Faromadan
Gift	Туҳфа	Tuhfa
Girl	Духтар	Dukhtar
Girlfriend	Дугона	Dugona
Give	Додан	Dodan
Glass	Шиша	Shisha
Glasses (eyeglasses)	Айнак	Aynak
Gloves	Дасткашак	Dastkashak
Glue	Ширеш	Shiresh
Go (walk)	Рафтан	Raftan
Go (drive)	Рафтан	Raftan
Go out	Ба берун рафтан	Ba berun raftan
God (deity)	Худо	Khudo
Gold	Тилло	Tillo
Good	Хуб	Khub
Government	Ҳукумат	Hukumat
Gram	Грамм	Gramm
Granddaughter	Набера (духтар)	Nabera (dukhtar)
Grandfather	Бобо	Bobo
Grandmother	Бибй	Bibi
Grandson	Набера (писар)	Nabera (pisar)
Grass	Алаф	Alaf
Grateful	Миннатдор	Minnatdor
Grave	Қабр	Qabr

English	Tajik	Pronunciation
Great (wonderful)	Олӣ	Oli
Green	Сабз	Sabz
Grey	Хокистарранг	Khokistarang
Grocery	Мағозаи хӯрока	Maghozai khuroka
Grow	Зиёд шудан	Ziyod shudan
Guaranteed	Кафолат дода мешавад	Kafolat doda meshavad
Guess	Тахмин кардан	Takhmin kardan
Guilty	Гунаҳкор	Gunahkor
Guitar	Гитар	Gitar
Gun	Таппонча	Tapponcha
Gym	Толори варзишӣ	Tolori varzishi

H

English	Tajik	Pronunciation
Hair	Мӯй	Muy
Hairbrush	Шона	Shona
Haircut	Мӯйгирӣ	Muygiri
Half	Нисф	Nisf
Hand	Даст	Dast
Handbag	Сумка	Sumka
Handkerchief	Рӯмолча	Rumolcha
Handmade	Сохти дастӣ	Sokhti dasti
Handsome	Зебо	Zebo
Happy	Хурсанд	Khursand
Hard (firm)	Сахт	Sakht
Hard-boiled	Сахт ҷӯшондашуда	Sakht jushondashuda
Hat	Кулоҳ	Kuloh
Have	Доштан	Doshtan
Have a cold	Шамол хӯрдан	Shamol khurdan
Have fun	Хурсандӣ кардан	Khursandi kardan
He	ӯ	u
Head	Сар	Sar
Headache	Сардард	Sardard
Headlights	Чароғҳои пеш	Charoghhoi pesh
Health	Саломатӣ	Salomati

English	Tajik	Pronunciation
Hear	Шунидан	Shunidan
Heart	Дил	Dil
Heat	Гармӣ	Garmi
Heated	Гарм кардашуда	Garm kardashuda
Heater	Гармкунак	Garmkunak
Heavy	Вазнин	Vaznin
Helmet	Тоскулоҳ	Toskuloh
Help	Ёрӣ додан	Yori dodan
Her (hers)	Аз они ӯ	Az oni u
Herb	Алаф	Alaf
Herbal	Алафӣ	Alafi
Here	Инҷо	Injo
High (steep)	Баланд	Baland
High school	Мактаби олӣ	Maktabi oli
Highway	Шоҳроҳ	Shohroh
Hike	Саёҳат кардан	Sayohat kardan
Hiking	Саёҳат кардан	Sayohat kardan
Hill	Теппа	Teppa
Hire	Иҷора гирифтан	Ijora giriftan
His	Аз они ӯ	Az oni u
History	Таърих	Ta'rikh
Holiday	Ид	Id
Holidays	Идҳо	Idho
Home	Хона	Khona
Honey	Асал	Asal
Horse	Асп	Asp
Hospital	Беморхона	Bemorkhona
Hot	Гарм	Garm
Hot water	Оби гарм	Obi garm
Hotel	Меҳмонхона	Mehmonkhona
Hour	Соат	Soat
House	Хона	Khona
How	Чӣ тавр	Chi tavr
How much	Чӣ қадар	Chi qadar
Hug	Оғӯш кардан	Oghush kardan
Humid	Намнок	Namnok

English	Tajik	Pronunciation
Hungry (famished)	Гурусна	Gurusna
Hurt	Зарар расондан	Zarar rasondan
Husband	Шавҳар	Shavhar

I

Ice	Ях	Yakh
Ice cream	Яхмос	Yakhmos
Identification	Муайянкунӣ	Muayyankunl
ID card	Ҳуҷҷати тасдиқкунанадаи шахсият	Hujjati tasdiqkunanadai shakhsiyat
Idiot	Ноқисулақл	Noqisulaql
If	Агар	Agar
Ill	Бемор	Bemor
Important	Муҳим	Muhim
Impossible	Ғайриимконпазир	Ghayriimkonpazir
In	Дар даруни	Dar daruni
(be) in a hurry	Саросема будан	Sarosema budan
In front of	Дар назди	Dar nazdi
Included	Дохил	Dokhil
Indoor	Дохили бино	Dokhili bino
Information	Маълумот	Ma'lumot
Ingredient	Таркиб	Tarkib
Injury	Осеб	Oseb
Innocent	Бегуноҳ	Begunoh
Inside	Дарун	Darun
Interesting	Аҷоиб	Ajoib
Invite	Даъват кардан	Da'vat kardan
Island	Ҷазира	Jazira
It	Он	On
Itch	Хоридан	Khoridan

50

English	Tajik	Pronunciation

J

Jacket	Болопӯш	Bolopush
Jail	Зиндон	Zindon
Jar	Зарф	Zarf
Jaw	Манаҳ	Manah
Jeep	Ҷип	Jip
Jewelry	Ҷавоҳирот	Javohirot जवाहरात
Job	Кор	Kor कार्य
Jogging	Давидан	Davidan
Joke	Шӯхй кардан	Shukhi kardan
Juice	Шарбат	Sharbat ✓
Jumper (cardigan)	Ҷемпер	Jemper

K

Key	Калид	Kalid
Keyboard	Клавиатура	Klaviatura Tastatur
Kilogram	Килограмм	Kilogram
Kilometer	Километр	Kilometr
Kind (sweet)	Меҳрубон	Mehrubon
Kindergarten	Боғчаи кӯдакон	Boghchai kudakon बगीचा
King	Подшоҳ	Podshoh बादशाह
Kiss	Бӯса кардан	Busa kardan se baiser
Kiss	Бӯса кардан	Busa kardan
Kitchen	Ошхона	Oshkhona खाना
Knee	Зону	Zonu जानु
Knife	Корд	Kord
Know	Донистан	Donistan ज्ञान

L

Lace	Банд	Band
Lake	Кул	Kul
Land	Замин	Zamin ज़मीन

51

English	Tajik	Pronunciation
Language	Забон	Zabon
Laptop	Лептоп	Leptop
Large	Калон	Kalon
Last (finale)	Охирон	Okhiron
Last (previously)	Гузашта	Guzashta
Law (edict)	Қонун	Qonun
Lawyer	Адвокат	Advokat
Lazy	Танбал	Tanbal
Leader	Пешво	Peshvo
Learn	Омӯхтан	Omukhtan
Leather	Чарм	Charm
Left (leftward)	Чап	Chap
Leg	Пой	Poy
Legal	Ҳуқуқӣ	Huquqi
Lemon	Лиму	Limu
Lemonade	Лимонад	Limonad
Lens	Линзаҳо	Linzaho
Lesbian	Лезбианка	Lezbianka
Less	Камтар	Kamtar
Letter (envelope)	Мактуб	Maktub
Lettuce	Карам	Karam
Liar	Дурӯғгу	Durughgu
Library	Китобхона	Kitobkhona
Lie (lying)	Хобидан	Khobidan
Lie (falsehood)	Дурӯғ гуфтан	Durugh guftan
Life	Зиндагӣ	Zindagi
Light	Равшан	Ravshan
Light (pale)	Равшан	Ravshan
Light (weightless)	Сабук	Sabuk
Light bulb	Фурӯзонак	Furuzonak
Lighter (ignited)	Оташфрӯзак	Otashfruzak
Like	Дӯст доштан	Dust doshtan
Lime	Оҳак	Ohak
Lips	Лабҳо	Labho
Lipstick	Лабсурхкунак	Labsurkhkunak
Liquor store	Мағозаи машрубот	Maghozai mashrubot

English	Tajik	Pronunciation
Listen	Гӯш кардан	Gush kardan
Little (few)	Кам	Kam
Little (tiny)	Хурд	Khurd
Live (occupy)	Зиндагӣ кардан	Zindagi kardan
Local	Маҳаллӣ	Mahalli
Lock	Қулф	Qulf
Locked	Қулф кардашуда	Qulf kardashuda
Long	Дароз	Daroz
Look	Нигоҳ кардан	Nigoh kardan
Look for	Кофтан	Koftan
Lose	Гум кардан	Gum kardan
Lost	Гумшуда	Gumshuda
(A) Lot	(B) Бисёр	(C) Bisyor
Loud	Баланд	Baland
Love	Дӯст доштан	Dust doshtan
Low	Паст	Past
Luck	Иқбол	Iqbol
Lucky	Хушбахт	Khushbakht
Luggage	Бағоҷ	Baghoj
Lump	Порча	Porcha
Lunch	Хӯроки нисфирӯзӣ	Khuroki nisfiruzi
Luxury	Шукуҳ	Shukuh

M

Machine	Мошина	Moshina
Magazine	Маҷалла	Majalla
Mail (mailing)	Бо почта равон кардан	Ba pochta ravon kardan
Mailbox	Қуттии почта	Quttii pochta
Main	Асосӣ	Asosi
Mainroad	Роҳи асосӣ	Rohi asosi
Make	Кардан	Kardan
Make-up	Ороиш	Oroish
Man	Одам, мард	Odam, mard
Many	Бисёр	Bisyor

English	Tajik	Pronunciation
Map	Харита	Kharita
Market	Бозор	Bozor
Marriage	Издивоҷ	Izdivoj
Marry	Издивоҷ кардан	Izdivoj kardan
Matches (matchbox)	Гугирд	Gugird
Mattress	Курпача	Kurpacha
Maybe	Шояд	Shoyad
Me	Ман	Man
Meal	Хӯрок	Khurok
Meat	Гушт	Gusht
Medicine (medicinals)	Дору	Doru
Meet	Вохӯрдан	Vokhurdan
Meeting	Вохӯрӣ	Vokhuri
Member	Узв	Uzv
Message	Паём	Payom
Metal	Метал	Metal
Meter	Метр	Metr
Microwave	Микромавҷӣ	Mikromavji
Midday	Нисфирӯзӣ	Nisfiruzi
Midnight	Нисфи шаб	Nisfi shab
Military	Ҳарбӣ	Harbi
Milk	Шир	Shir
Millimeter	Милиметр	Milimetr
Minute (moment)	Дақиқа	Daqiqa
Mirror	Оина	Oina
Miss (lady)	Хонум	Khonum
Miss (mishap)	Ба ҳадаф нарасидан	Ba hadaf narasidan
Mistake	Хато	Khato
Mobile phone	Телефони мобилӣ	Telefoni mobili
Modern	Муосир	Muosir
Money	Пул	Pul
Month	Моҳ	Moh
More	Бисёртар	Bisyortar
Morning	Саҳар	Sahar
Mosquito	Магас	Magas
Motel	Меҳмонхона	Mehmonkhona

English	Tajik	Pronunciation
Mother	Модар	Modar
Mother-in-law	Хушдоман	Khushdoman
Motorbike	Мотосикл	Motosikl
Motorboat	Қаиқи муҳаррикдор	Qaiqi muharrikdor
Mountain	Кӯҳ	Kuh
Mountain range	Силсилакӯҳ	Silsilakuh
Mouse	Муш	Mush
Mouth	Даҳон	Dahon
Movie	Синамо	Sinamo
Mr.	Ҷаноб	Janob
Mrs./Ms	Хонум	Khonum
Mud	Лой	Loy
Murder	Куштор	Kushtor
Muscle	Мушак	Mushak
Museum	Осорхона	Osorkhona
Music	Мусиқӣ	Musiqi
Mustard	Хардал	Khardal
Mute	Гунг	Gung
My	Аз они ман	Az oni man

N

Nail clippers	Нохунгирак	Nokhungirak
Name (moniker)	Ном	Nom
Name (term)	Ном	Nom
Name (surname)	Ном	Nom
Napkin	Дастпоккунак	Dastpokkunak
Nature	Табиат	Tabiat
Nausea	Дилбеҳузурӣ	Dilbehuzuri
Near (close)	Наздик	Nazdik
Nearest	Наздиктарин	Nazdiktarin
Necessity	Зарурат	Zarurat
Neck	Гардан	Gardan
Necklace	Гарданбанд	Gardanband
Need	Ҳоҷҷат	Hojjat
Needle (stitch)	Сӯзан	Suzan

English	Tajik	Pronunciation
Negative	Манфӣ	Manfi
Neither...nor...	На... на....	Na... na....
Net	Тур	Tur
Never	Ҳеҷгоҳ	Hejgoh
New	Нав	Nav
News	Хабарнав	Khabarnav
Newspaper	Рӯзнома	Ruznoma
Next (ensuing)	Навбатӣ	Navbati
Next to	Дар назди	Dar nazdi
Nice	Хуб	Khub
Nickname	Лақаб	Laqab
Night	Шаб	Shab
Nightclub	Клуб	Klub
No	Не	Ne
Noisy	Серғавғо	Serghavgho
None	Ҳеҷ кадом	Hej kadom
Nonsmoking	Тамоку намекашида	Tamoku namekashida
Noon	Нисфирӯзӣ	Nisfiruzi
North	Шимол	Shimol
Nose	Бинӣ	Bini
Not	Не	Ne
Notebook	Дафтар	Daftar
Nothing	Ҳеҷ чиз	Hej chiz
Now	Ҳозир	Hozir
Number	Рақам	Raqam
Nurse	Ҳамшира	Hamshira
Nut	Чормағз	Chormaghz

O

Ocean	Уқёнус	Uqyonus
Off (strange)	Хомӯш	Khomush
Office	Идора	Idora
Often	Зуд-зуд	Zud-zud
Oil (oily)	Равған	Ravghan
Old	Кӯҳна	Kuhna

English	Tajik	Pronunciation
On	Даргирондан	Dargironda
On time	Саривақт	Sarivaqt
Once	Як бор	Yak bor
One	Як	Yak
One-way	Як тарафа	Yak tarafa
Only	Танхо	Tanho
Open	Кушодан	Kushodan
Operation (process)	Кор	Kor
Operator	Оператор	Operator
Opinion	Ақида	Aqida
Opposite	Муқобил	Muqobil
Or	Ё	Yo
Orange (citrus)	Афлесун	Aflesun
Orange (color)	Афлесунй	Aflesuni
Orchestra	Оркестр	Orkestr
Order	Фармон	Farmon
Order	Тартиб	Tartib
Ordinary	Оддй	Oddi
Original	Аслй	Asli
Other	Дигар	Digar
Our	Аз мо	Az mo
Outside	Берун	Berun
Oven	Танӯр	Tanur
Overnight	Шабонарӯз	Shabonaruz
Overseas	Хориҷа	Khorija
Owner	Соҳиб	Sohib
Oxygen	Оксиген	Oksigen

P

Package	Баста	Basta
Packet	Пакет	Paket
Padlock	Қулф	Qulf
Page	Саҳифа	Sahifa
Pain	Дард	Dard
Painful	Дарднок	Dardnok

English	Tajik	Pronunciation
Painkiller	Пасткунандаи дард	Pastkunandai dar
Painter	Рассом	Rassom
Painting (canvas)	Расм	Rasm
Painting (the art)	Расм	Rasm
Pair	Ҷуфт	Juft
Pan	Тоба	Toba
Pants (slacks)	Шим	Shim
Paper	Қоғаз	Qoghaz
Paperwork	Кори қоғазӣ	Kori qoghazi
Parents	Волидайн	Volidayn
Park	Парк	Park
Park (parking)	Таваққуф кардан	Tavaquf kardan
Part (piece)	Қисм	Qism
Part-time	Нимавақт	Nimavaqt
Party (celebration)	Шабнишинӣ	Shabnishini
Party (political)	Ҳизб	Hizb
Pass	Гузаштан	Guzashtan
Passenger	Мусофир	Musofir
Passport	Шиноснома	Shinosnoma
Past (ago)	Гузашта	Guzashta
Path	Роҳ	Roh
Pay	Пардохт кардан	Pardokht kardan
Payment	Пардохт	Pardokht
Peace	Сулҳ	Sulh
Peach	Шафтолу	Shaftolu
Peanut	Арахис	Arakhis
Pear	Нок	Nok
Pedal	Педал	Pedal
Pedestrian	Роҳгузар	Rohguzar
Pen	Қалам	Qalam
Pencil	Қалам	Qalam
People	Одамон	Odamon
Pepper (peppery)	Қаланфур	Qalanfur
Per	Ҳар як	Har yak
Per cent	Фоиз	Foiz
Perfect	Мукаммал	Mukammal

English	Tajik	Pronunciation
Performance	Иҷро	Ijro
Perfume	Хушбӯй	Khushbuy
Permission (permit)	Иҷозат	Ijozat
Person	Одам	Odam
Petrol	Сӯзишворӣ	Sūzishvori
Petrol station	Нуқтаи сӯзишворӣ	Nuqtai suzishvori
Pharmacy	Дорухона	Dorukhona
Phone book	Китоби телефон	Kitobi telefon
Photo	Сурат	Surat
Photographer	Суратгир	Suratgir
Pigeon	Кабутар	Kabutar
Pie	Пирог	Pirog
Piece	Қисм	Qism
Pig	Хук	Khuk
Pill	Дору	Doru
Pillow	Таксарӣ	Taksari
Pillowcase	Ҷилди таксарӣ	Jildi taksari
Pink	Гулобӣ	Gulobi
Place	Ҷой	Joy
Plane	Тайёра	Tayyora
Planet	Сайёра	Sayyora
Plant	Растанӣ	Rastani
Plastic	Пластикӣ	Plastiki
Plate	Табақ	Tabaq
Play (strum)	Навохтан	Navokhtan
Play (theatrical)	Бозӣ кардан	Bozi kardan
Plug (stopper)	Васл кардан	Vasl kardan
Plug (socket)	Васлак	Vaslak
Plum	Олу	Olu
Pocket	Кисса	Kissa
Point	Нуқта	Nuqta
Poisonous	Заҳрнок	Zahrnok
Police	Пулис	Pulis
Police officer	Афсари пулис	Afsari pulis
Police station	Идораи пулис	Idorai pulis
Politics	Сиёсат	Siyosat

English	Tajik	Pronunciation
Pollution	Ифлоскунй	Ifloskuni
Pool (basin)	Ҳавз	Havz
Poor	Камбағал	Kambaghal
Popular	Машхур	Mashhur
Pork	Гушти хук	Gushti khuk
Port (dock)	Порт	Port
Positive	Мусбат	Musbat
Possible	Имконпазир	Imkonpazir
Postcard	Қоғази хатнависй	Qoghazi khatnavisi
Post office	Почта	Pochta
Pot (kettle)	Чойник	Choynik
Potato	Картошка	Kartoshka
Pottery	Маҳсулоти кӯлолгарй	Mahsuloti kulolgari
Pound (ounces)	Фунт	Funt
Poverty	Камбизоатй	Kambizoati
Powder	Хока	Khoka
Power	Қувват	Quvvat
Prayer	Дуо	Duo
Prefer	Хостан	Khostan
Pregnant	Ҳомиладор	Homilador
Prepare	Тайёр кардан	Tayyor kardan
Prescription	Дорухат	Dorukhat
Present (treat)	Туҳфа	Tuhfa
Present (now)	Ҳозир	Hozir
President	Президент	Prezident
Pressure	Фишор	Fishor
Pretty	Зебо	Zebo
Price	Нарх	Narkh
Priest	Руҳонй	Ruhoni
Printer (printing)	Принтер	Printer
Prison	Маҳбас	Mahbas
Private	Хусусй	Khususi
Produce	Истеҳсол кардан	Istehsol kardan
Profit	Фоида	Foida
Program	Барнома	Barnoma
Promise	Ваъда додан	Va'da dodan

English	Tajik	Pronunciation
Protect	Муҳофизат кардан	Muhofizat kardan
Pub	Майхона	Maykhona
Public toilet	Ҳоҷатхона	Hojatkhona
Pull	Кашидн	Kashidn
Pump	Насос	Nasos
Pumpkin	Каду	Kadu
Pure	Тоза	Toza
Purple	Бунафшаранг	Bunafsharang
Purse	Ҷувздон	Juvzdon
Push	Тела додан	Tela dodan
Put	Гузоштан	Guzoshtan

Q

Quality	Сифат	Sifat
Quarter	Чоряк	Chiryak
Queen	Малика	Malika
Question	Савол	Savol
Queue	Қатор	Qator
Quick	Тез	Tez
Quiet	Ором	Orom
Quit	Тарк кардан	Tark kardan

R

Rabbit	Харгӯш	Khargush
Race (running)	Мусобиқа	Musobiqa
Radiator	Радиатор	Radiator
Radio	Радио	Radio
Rain	Борон	Boron
Raincoat	Боронй	Boroni
Rare (exotic)	Нодир	Nodir
Rare (unique)	Нодир	Nodir
Rash	Донача	Donacha
Raspberry	Тамашк	Tamashk
Rat	Каламуш	Kalamush

English	Tajik	Pronunciation
Raw	Хом	Khoum
Razor	Покy	Poku
Read	Хондан	Khondan
Reading	Хондан	Khondan
Ready	Тайёр	Tayyor
Rear (behind)	Пас	Pas
Reason	Сабаб	Sabab
Receipt	Расид	Rasid
Recently	Ба наздикй	Ba nazdiki
Recomment	Тавсия	Tavsiya
Record (music)	Сабт кардан	Sabt kardan
Recycle	Дубора истифода бурдан	Dubora istifoda burdan
Red	Сурх	Surkh
Refrigerator	Яхдон	Yakhdon
Refund	Ҷуброн кардан	Jubron kardan
Refuse	Рад кардан	Rad kardan
Regret	Пушаймон шудан	Pushaymon shudan
Relationship	Муносибат	Munosibat
Relax	Истироҳат кардан	Istirohat kardan
Relic	Чизи азизу гаронбаҳо	Chizi azizu garonbaho
Religion	Дин	Din
Religious	Динй	Dini
Remote	Дурдаст	Durdast
Rent	Иҷора	Ijora
Repair	Таъмир	Ta'mir
Reservation (reserving)	Брон	Bron
Rest	Роҳат кардан	Rohat kardan
Restaurant	Тарабхона	Tarabkhona
Return (homecoming)	Баргаштан	Bargashtan
Return (returning)	Баргаштан	Bargashtan
Review	Барраcй	Barrasi
Rhythm	Назм	Nazm
Rib	Қабурға	Qaburgha
Rice	Биринҷ	Birinj

English	Tajik	Pronunciation
Rich (prosperous)	Бой	Boy
Ride	Рондан	Rondan
Ride (riding)	Рондан	Rondan
Right (appropriate)	Муносиб	Munosib
Right (rightward)	Рост	Rost
Ring (bauble)	Ҳалқа	Halqa
Ring (ringing)	Занг задан	Zang zadan
Rip-off	Даридан	Daridan
River	Дарё	Daryo
Road	Дар	Dar
Rob	Дуздидан	Duzdidan
Robbery	Дузди	Duzdi
Rock	Харсанг	Kharsang
Romantic	Романтикй	Romantiki
Room (accommodation)	Ҳучра	Hujra
Room (chamber)	Ҳучра	Hujra
Room number	Рақами ҳучра	Raqami hujra
Rope	Банд	Band
Round	Гирд	Gird
Route	Маршрут	Marshrut
Rug	Қолин	Qolin
Ruins	Харобахо	Kharobaho
Rule	Қоида	Qoida
Rum	Ром	Rom
Run	Давидан	Davidan

S

Sad	Зиқ	Ziq
Safe	Бехатар	Bekhatar
Salad	Салат	Salat
Sale (special)	Савдо	Savdo
Sales tax	Андоз аз савдо	Andoz az savdo
Salmon	Озодмоҳй	Ozodmohi
Salt	Намак	Namak

English	Tajik	Pronunciation
Same	Якхела	Yakkhela
Sand	Рег	Reg
Sandal	Шиппак	Shippak
Sauce	Соус	Sous
Saucepan	Дегча	Degcha
Sauna	Сауна	Sauna
Say	Гуфтан	Guftan
Scarf	Рӯймол	Ruymol
School	Мактаб	Maktab
Science	Илм	Ilm
Scientist	Олим	Olim
Scissors	Қайчи	Qaychi
Sea	Баҳр	Bahr
Seasickness	Касалии баҳр	Kasalii bahr
Season	Мавсим	Mavsim
Seat	Ҷои нишаст	Joi nishast
Seatbelt	Тасмаи бехатарй	Tasmai bekhatari
Second (moment)	Сония	Soniya
Second	Дуюм	Duyum
See	Дидан	Didan
Selfish	Худписанд	Khudpisand
Sell	Фурӯхтан	Furukhtan
Send	Фиристондан	Firistondan
Sensible	Маънодор	Ma'nodor
Sensual	Ҳиссӣ	Hissi
Seperate	Ҷудо кардан	Judo kardan
Serious	Ҷиддӣ	Jiddi
Service	Хизмат	Khizmat
Several	Якчанд	Yakchand
Sew	Дӯхтан	Dukhtan
Sex	Ҷинс	Jins
Sexism	Ҷинсӣ	Jinsi
Sexy	Санобар	Sanobar
Shade (shady)	Соя	Soya
Shampoo	Шампун	Shampun
Shape	Шакл	Shakl

English	Tajik	Pronunciation
Share (sharing)	Тақсим кардан	Taqsim kardan
Share (allotment)	Тақсим кардан	Taqsim kardan
Shave	Тарошидан	Taroshidan
Shaving cream	Крем барои тарошидан	Krem baroi taroshidan
She	ӯ	ū
Sheet (linens)	Чодир	Chodir
Ship	Киштӣ	Kishti
Shirt	Курта	Kurta
Shoes	Пойафзол	Poyafzol
Shoot	Парондан	Parondan
Shop	Мағоза	Maghoza
Shop	Мағоза	Maghoza
Shopping center	Маркази савдо	Markazi savdo
Short (low)	Кӯтоҳ	Kutoh
Shortage	Камбудӣ	Kambudi
Shorts	Шортик	Shortik
Shoulder	Китф	Kitf
Shout	Дод задан	Dod zadan
Show	Нишон додан	Nishon dodan
Show	Нишон додан	Nishon dodan
Shower	Душ	Dush
Shut	Пӯшидан	Pushidan
Shy	Шармгин	Sharmgin
Sick	Касал	Kasal
Side	Тараф	Taraf
Sign	Аломат	Alomat
Sign (signature)	Имзо кардан	Imzo kardan
Signature	Имзо	Imzo
Silk	Абрешим	Abreshim
Silver	Нуқра	Nuqra
Similar	Монанд	Monand
Simple	Осон	Oson
Since	Аз вақте	Az vaqte
Sing	Сароидан	Saroidan
Singer	Сароянда	Saroyanda

English	Tajik	Pronunciation
Single (individual)	Танхо	Tanxo
Sister	Хоҳар	Khohar
Sit	Шиштан	Shishtan
Size (extent)	Андоза	Andoza
Skin	Пӯст	Pust
Skirt	Юбка	Yubka
Sky	Осмон	Osmon
Sleep	Хоб кардан	Khob kardan
Sleepy	Хоболул	Khobolul
Slice	Порча	Porcha
Slow	Оҳиста	Ohista
Slowly	Оҳиста	Ohista
Small	Хурд	Khurd
Smell	Бӯй	Buy
Smile	Табассум	Tabassum
Smoke	Тамоку кашидан	Tamoku kashidan
Snack	Хӯриш	Khurish
Snake	Мор	Mor
Snow	Барф	Barf
Soap	Собун	Sobun
Socks	Ҷӯраб	Jurab
Soda	Сода	Soda
Soft-drink	Нӯшокӣ	Nushoki
Some	Баъзе	Ba'ze
Someone	Касе	Kase
Something	Чизе	Chize
Son	Писар	Pisar
Song	Суруд	Surud
Soon	Ба наздикӣ	Ba nazdiki
Sore	Дард	Dard
Soup	Шурбо	Shurbo
South	Ҷануб	Janub
Specialist	Мутахассис	Mutakhassis
Speed (rate)	Суръат	Sur'at
Spinach	Исфаноҷ	Isfanoj
Spoiled (rotten)	Вайроншуда	Vayronshuda

English	Tajik	Pronunciation
Spoke	Гап зад	Gap zad
Spoon	Қошуқ	Qoshuq
Sprain	Ёзондан	Yozondan
Spring (prime)	Баҳор	Bahor
Square (town center)	Майдон	Maydon
Stadium	Варзишгоҳ	Varzishgoh
Stamp	Муҳр	Muhr
Star	Ситора	Sitora
Star sign	Имзои ситора	Imzoi sitora
Start	Оғоз	Oghoz
Station	Истгоҳ	Istgoh
Statue	Пайкара	Paykara
Stay (sleepover)	Истодан	Istodan
Steak	Нимбирён	Nimbiryon
Steal	Дуздидан	Duzdidan
Steep	Нишеб	Nisheb
Step	Қадам	Qadam
Stolen	Дуздидашуда	Duzdidashuda
Stomach	Меъда	Me'da
Stomach ache	Дарди меъда	Dardi me'da
Stone	Санг	Sang
Stop (station)	Истгоҳ	Istgoh
Stop (halt)	Истодан	Istodan
Stop (avoid)	Манъ кардан	Man' kardan
Storm	Шамол	Shamol
Story	Ҳикоя	Hikoya
Stove	Танур	Tanur
Straight	Рост	Rost
Strange	Аҷиб	Ajib
Stranger	Ношинос	Noshinos
Strawberry	Тути заминӣ	Tuti zamini
Street	Кӯча	Kucha
String	Сатр	Satr
Stroller	Арбача	Arbacha
Strong	Боқувват	Boquvvat
Stubborn	Якрав	Yakrav

English	Tajik	Pronunciation
Student	Донишчӯ	Donishju
Studio	Студио	Studio
Stupid	Беақл	Beaql
Suburb	Назди шаҳр	Nazdi shahr
Subway (underground)	Метро	Metro
Sugar	Шакар	Shakar
Suitcase	Ҷомадон	Jomadon
Summer	Тобистон	Tobiston
Sun	Офтоб	Oftob
Sun block	Крем	Krem
Sunburn	Сӯхта	Sukhta
Sunglasses	Айнак	Aynak
Sunny	Офтобӣ	Oftobi
Sunrise	Тулӯи офтоб	Tului oftob
Sunset	Ғуруби офтоб	Ghurubi oftob
Supermarket	Супермаркет	Supermarket
Surf	Серфинг кардан	Serfing kardan
Surprise	Сюрприз	Syurpriz
Sweater	Свитер	Sviter
Sweet	Ширин	Shirin
Swelling	Варам	Varam
Swim	Шино кардан	Shino kardan
Swiming pool	Ҳавз	Havz
Swimsuit	Либоси оббозӣ	Libosi obbozi

T

Table	Ҷадвал	Jadval
Tablecloth	Дастархон	Dastarkhon
Tall	Баланд	Baland
Take	Гирифтан	Giriftan
Take photos	Сурат гирифтан	Surat giriftan
Talk	Мулоқот кардан	Muloqot kardan
Tap	Ҷуммак	Jummak
Tap water	Қуммаки об	Qummaki ob

68

English	Tajik	Pronunciation
Tasty	Болаззат	Bolazzat
Tea	Чой	Choy
Teacher	Муаллим	Muallim
Team	Гурӯҳ	Guruh
Teaspoon	Қошуқ	Qoshuq
Teeth	Дандон	Dandon
Telephone	Телефон	Telefon
Television	Телевизор	Televizor
Tell	Гуфтан	Guftan
Temperature (feverish)	Ҳарорат	Harorat
Temperature (degrees)	Ҳарорат	Harorat
Terrible	Бад	Bad
Thank	Ташаккур кардан	Tashakkur kardan
That (one)	Он	On
Theater	Театр	Teatr
Their	Аз онҳо	Az onho
There	Дар онҷо	Dar onjo
Thermometer	Ҳароратсанҷ	Haroratsanj
They	Онҳо	Onho
Thick	Ғафс	Ghafs
Thief	Дузд	Duzd
Thin	Тунук	Tunuk
Think	Фикр кардан	Fikr kardan
Third	Сеюм	Seyum
Thirsty (parched)	Ташна	Tashna
This (one)	Ин	In
Throat	Гулӯ	Gulu
Ticket	Чипта	Chipta
Tight	Зич	Zich
Time	Вақт	Vaqt
Time difference	Фарқияти вақт	Farqiyati vaqt
Tin (aluminium can)	Қуттӣ	Qutti
Tiny	Хурд	Khurd
Tip (tipping)	Пешпо хӯрдан	Peshpo khurdan

English	Tajik	Pronunciation
Tire	Монда шудан	Monda shudan
Tired	Монда шуда	Monda shuda
Tissues	Қоғази тунук	Qoghazi tunuk
To	Ба	Ba
Toast (toasting)	Тост	Tost
Toaster	Тостер	Toster
Tobacco	Тамоку	Tamoku
Today	Имрӯз	Imruz
Toe	Ангушти пой	Angushti poy
Together	Якҷоя	Yakjoya
Toilet	Ҳоҷатхона	Hojatkhona
Toilet paper	Қоғази ташноб	Qoghazi tashnob
Tomato	Помидор	Pomidor
Tomorrow	Пагоҳ	Pagoh
Tonight	Имшаб	Imshab
Too (additionally)	Ҳам	Ham
Too (excessively)	Хеле	Khele
Tooth	Дандон	Dandon
Toothbrush	Чӯткаи дандоншӯй	Chutkai dandonshui
Toothpaste	Хамираи дандоншӯй	Khamirai dandonshui
Touch	Ламс кардан	Lams kardan
Tour	Саёҳат кардан	Sayohat kardan
Tourist	Сайёҳ	Sayyoh
Towards	Ба	Ba
Towel	Сачоқ	Sachoq
Tower	Бурҷ	Burj
Track (pathway)	Роҳрав	Rohrav
Track (racing)	Таъқиб кардан	Ta'qib kardan
Trade (trading)	Савдо	Savdo
Trade (career)	Савдо	Savdo
Traffic	Ҳаракат	Harakat
Traffic light	Светофор	Svetofor
Trail	Асар	Asar
Train	Қаттора	Qattora
Train station	Истгоҳи роҳи оҳан	Istgohi rohi ohan
Tram	Трамвай	Tramvay

English	Tajik	Pronunciation
Translate	Тарҷума кардан	Tarjuma kardan
Translation	Тарҷума	Tarjuma
Transport	Интиқол дода	Intiqol doda
Travel	Сафар кардан	Safar kardan
Tree	Дарахт	Darakht
Trip (expedition)	Сайр кардан	Sayr kardan
Truck	Мошини боркаш	Moshini borkash
Trust	Мовар кардан	Mosvar kardan
Try (trying)	Кӯшиш кардан	Kushish kardan
Try (sip)	Чашидан	Chashidan
T-shirt	Футболка	Futbolka
Turkey	Туркия	Turkiya
Turn	Гаштан	Gashtan
TV	ТВ	TV
Tweezers	Мӯйчинак	Muychinak
Twice	Ду карата	Du karata
Twins	Дугоник	Dugonik
Two	Ду	Du
Type	Навъ	Nav'
Typical	Оддӣ	Oddi

U

Umbrella	Шамсия	Shamsiya
Uncomfortable	Нороҳат	Norohat
Understand	Фаҳмидан	Fahmidan
Underwear	Тагпӯш	Tagpush
Unfair	Беадолатона	Beadolatona
Until	То	To
Unusual	Ғайриоддӣ	Ghayrioddi
Up	Боло	Bolo
Uphill	Кӯтал	Kutal
Urgent	Фаврӣ	Favri
Useful	Фоидаовар	Foidaovar

English	Tajik	Pronunciation

V

Vacation	Таътил	Ta'til
Valuable	Арзишманд	Arzishmand
Value	Арзиш	Arzish
Van	Ароба	Aroba
Vegetable	Сабзавот	Sabzavot
Vegeterian	Гиёҳхорон	Giyohkhoron
Venue	Макон	Makon
Very	Хеле	Khele
Video recorder	Видео сабткунанда	Video sab kunanda
View	Намоиш	Namoish
Village	Деҳа	Deha
Vinegar	Сирко	Sirko
Virus	Вирус	Virus
Visit	Ташриф овардан	Tashrif ovardan
Visit	Ташриф	Tashrif
Voice	Овоз	Ovoz
Vote	Овоз додан	Ovoz dodan

W

Wage	Музд	Muzd
Wait	Интизор будан	Intizor budam
Waiter	Пешхизмат	Peshkhizmat
Waiting room	Ҳуҷраи интизорӣ	Hujrai intizori
Wake (someone) up	Бедор кардан	Bedor kardan
Walk	Роҳ гаштан	Roh gashtan
Want	Хостан	Khostan
War	Ҷанг	Jang
Wardrobe	Ҷевони либос	Jevoni libos
Warm	Гарм	Garm
Warn	Огоҳ кардан	Ogoh kardan
Wash (bathe)	Шӯстан	Shustan
Wash (scrub)	Шӯстан	Shustan

English	Tajik	Pronunciation
Wash cloth	Матои шӯстанӣ	Matoi shustani
Washing machine	Мошинаи либосшӯй	Moshinai libosshui
Watch	Тамошо кардан	Tamosho kardan
Watch	Соат	Soat
Water	Об	Ob
Water bottle	Қуттии об	Quttii ob
Watermelon	Харбӯза	Kharbuza
Waterproof	Обногузар	Obnoguzar
Wave	Мавҷ	Mavj
Way	Роҳ	Roh
We	Мо	Mo
Wealthy	Сарватманд	Sarvatmand
Wear	Пӯшидан	Pushidan
Weather	Обу ҳаво	Obu havo
Wedding	Тӯй	Tuy
Week	Хафта	Khafta
Weekend	Охири ҳафта	Okhiri hafta
Weigh	Бар кашидан	Bar kashidan
Weight	Вазн	Vazn
Weights	Вазн	Vazn
Welcome	Хӯш омадед	Khush omaded
Well	Чоҳ	Choh
West	Ғарб	Gharb
Wet	Тар	Tar
What	Чӣ	Chi
Wheel	Чарх	Charkh
Wheelchair	Аробача	Arobacha
When	Кай	Kay
Where	Дар куҷо	Dar kujo
Which	Кадом	Kadom
White	Сафед	Safed
Who	Кӣ	Ki
Why	Барои чӣ	Baroi chi
Wide	Кушод	Kushod
Wife	Зан	Zan
Win	Бурд кардан	Burd kardan

73

English	Tajik	Pronunciation
Wind	Шамол	Shamol
Window	Тиреза	Tireza
Wine	Май	May
Winner	Ғолиб	Gholib
Winter	Зимистон	Zimiston
Wish	Орзу кардан	Orzu kardan
With	Бо	Bo
Within (until)	Дар чорчӯбаи	Dar chorchubai
Without	Бе	Be
Wonderful	Олиҷаноб	Olijanob
Wood	Тахта	Takhta
Wool	Пашм	Pashm
Word	Калима	Kalima
Work	Кор	Kor
World	Ҷаҳон	Jahon
Worried	Нигарон	Nigaron
Wrist	Банди даст	Bandi dast
Write	Навиштан	Navishtan
Writer	Навмсанда	Navmsanda
Wrong	Нодуруст	Nodurust

Y

Year	Сол	Sol
Years	Солхо	Solho
Yellow	Зард	Zard
Yes	Ҳа	Ha
Yesterday	Дирӯз	Diruz
(Not) yet	Ҳанӯз	Hanuz
You	Ту	Tu
You	Шумо	Shumo
Young	Ҷавон	Javon
Your	Аз ту	Az tu

English	Tajik	Pronunciation

Z

Zipper	Занҷирак	Zanjirak
Zoo	Боғи ҳайвонҳо	Boghi hayvonho
Zucchini	Кадуи сабз	Kadui sabz

b. Tajik-English Dictionary

Tajik	Pronunciation	English

A

Tajik	Pronunciation	English
Аз вақте	Az vaqte	Since
Аз мо	Az mo	Our
Аз они ӯ	Az oni u	Her (hers)
Аз они ӯ	Az oni u	His
Аз они ман	Az oni man	My
Аз онхо	Az onho	Their
Аз ту	Az tu	Your
Айнак	Aynak	Glasses (eyeglasses)
Айнак	Aynak	Sunglasses
Ақида	Aqida	Opinion
Алаф	Alaf	Grass
Алаф	Alaf	Herb
Алафй	Alafi	Herbal
Аллакай	Allakay	Already
Аллергия	Allergiya	Allergy
Аломат	Alomat	Sign
Англисй	Anglisi	English
Ангушт	Angusht	Finger
Ангушти пой	Angushti poy	Toe
Андоз аз савдо	Andoz az savdo	Sales tax
Андоза	Andoza	Size (extent)
Аниқ	Aniq	Exactly
Арахис	Arakhis	Peanut
Арбача	Arbacha	Stroller
Арзиш	Arzish	Value
Арзишманд	Arzishmand	Valuable
Арзон	Arzon	Cheap
Ароба	Aroba	Van
Аробача	Arobacha	Wheelchair
Асал	Asal	Honey
Асар	Asar	Trail

76

Tajik	Pronunciation	English
Аслй	Asli	Original
Асосй	Asosi	Main
Асп	Asp	Horse
Аспирин	Aspirin	Aspirin
Афлесун	Aflesun	Orange (citrus)
Афлесунй	Aflesuni	Orange (color)
Афсари пулис	Afsari pulis	Police officer
Афтидан	Aftidan	Fall (falling)
Аҷиб	Ajib	Strange
Аҷоиб	Ajoib	Interesting

Б

Ба	Ba	To
Ба	Ba	Towards
Ба берун рафтан	Ba berun raftan	Go out
Ба наздикй	Ba nazdiki	Recently
Ба наздикй	Ba nazdiki	Soon
Ба пеш	Ba pesh	Ahead
Ба ҳадаф нарасидан	Ba hadaf narasidan	Miss (mishap)
Бағоҷ	Baghoj	Baggage
Бағоҷ	Baghoj	Luggage
Бад	Bad	Bad
Бад	Bad	Terrible
Бадан	Badan	Body
Баланд	Baland	High (steep)
Баланд	Baland	Loud
Баланд	Baland	Tall
Банан	Banan	Banana
Банд	Band	Lace
Банд	Band	Rope
Банди даст	Bandi dast	Wrist
Банкомат	Bankomat	ATM
Бар кашидан	Bar kashidan	Weigh
Барабан	Baraban	Drums
Барвақт	Barvaqt	Early

Tajik	Pronunciation	English
Баргаштан	Bargashtan	Return (homecoming)
Баргаштан	Bargashtan	Return (returning)
Барқ	Barq	Electricity
Барнома	Barnoma	Program
Бародар	Barodar	Brother
Барои он	Baroi on	Because
Барои чй	Baroi chi	Why
Баромад	Baromad	Exit
Баромадан	Baromadan	Climb
Баррасй	Barrasi	Review
Барф	Barf	Snow
Баста	Basta	Package
Батарея	Batareya	Battery
Баҳор	Bahor	Spring (prime)
Баҳр	Bahr	Sea
Баҳраманд шудан	Bahramand shudan	Enjoy (enjoying)
Баҳс кардан	Bahs kardan	Argue
Баъд аз	Ba'd az	After
Баъзе	Ba'ze	Some
Бе	Be	Without
Беадолатона	Beadolatona	Unfair
Беақл	Beaql	Stupid
Бегоҳ	Begoh	Evening
Бегуноҳ	Begunoh	Innocent
Бедор кардан	Bedor kardan	Wake (someone) up
Бекон	Bekon	Bacon
Бекор кардан	Bekor kardan	Cancel
Бемор	Bemor	Ill
Беморхона	Bemorkhona	Hospital
Берун	Berun	Outside
Бехатар	Bekhatar	Safe
Беҳтарин	Behtarin	Best
Бибй	Bibi	Grandmother
Биёбон	Biyobon	Desert
Бинй	Bini	Nose
Бино	Bino	Building

Tajik	Pronunciation	English
Бирён кардан	Biron kardan	Fry
Биринҷ	Birinj	Rice
Бисёр	Bisyor	Many
Бисёртар	Bisyortar	More
Бӯй	Buy	Smell
Бо	Bo	With
Бо почта равон кардан	Ba pochta ravon kardan	Mail (mailing)
Бобо	Bobo	Grandfather
Боғ	Bogh	Garden
Боғи ҳайвонҳо	Boghi hayvonho	Zoo
Боғчаи кӯдакон	Boghchai kudakon	Kindergarten
Бозӣ	Bozi	Game (match-up)
Бозӣ	Bozi	Game (event)
Бозӣ кардан	Bozi kardan	Play (theatrical)
Бозор	Bozor	Market
Бой	Boy	Rich (prosperous)
Боқувват	Boquvvat	Strong
Болаззат	Bolazzat	Tasty
Болиғ,	Boligh	Adult
Боло	Bolo	Up
Болопӯш	Bolopush	Jacket
Бонк	Bonk	Bank
Борон	Boron	Rain
Боронӣ	Boroni	Raincoat
Борхалта	Borkhalta	Backpack
Брон	Bron	Reservation (reserving)
Бӯса кардан	Busa kardan	Kiss
Бӯса кардан	Busa kardan	Kiss
Будан	Budan	Be
Бунафшаранг	Bunafsharang	Purple
Бурд кардан	Burd kardan	Win
Буридан	Buridan	Cut
Бурҷ	Burj	Tower
Бучули пой	Bujuli poy	Ankle

Tajik	Pronunciation	English

В

Tajik	Pronunciation	English
Ва	Va	And
Вазн	Vazn	Weight
Вазн	Vazn	Weights
Вазнин	Vaznin	Heavy
Вайроншуда	Vayronshuda	Spoiled (rotten)
Вақт	Vaqt	Time
Вақти пурра	Vaqti purra	Full-time
Варам	Varam	Swelling
Варзишгоҳ	Varzishgoh	Stadium
Васл кардан	Vasl kardan	Plug (stopper)
Васлак	Vaslak	Plug (socket)
Ваъда додан	Va'da dodan	Promise
Велосипед	Velosiped	Bicycle
Велосипед	Velosiped	Bike
Видео сабткунанда	Video sab kunanda	Video recorder
Вирус	Virus	Virus
Волидайн	Volidayn	Parents
Ворид	Vorid	Entry
Вохӯрӣ	Vokhuri	Appointment
Вохӯрӣ	Vokhuri	Meeting
Вохӯрдан	Vokhurdan	Meet

Г

Tajik	Pronunciation	English
Гап зад	Gap zad	Spoke
Гардан	Gardan	Neck
Гарданбанд	Gardanband	Necklace
Гармӣ	Garmi	Heat
Гарм	Garm	Hot
Гарм	Garm	Warm
Гарм кардашуда	Garm kardashuda	Heated
Гармкунак	Garmkunak	Heater
Гаштан	Gashtan	Turn

Tajik	Pronunciation	English
Гелос	Gelos	Cherry
Гиёҳхорон	Giyohkhoron	Vegeterian
Гирд	Gird	Round
Гирифта	Girifta	Get
Гирифтан	Giriftan	Take
Гирифтани бағоч	Giriftani baghoj	Baggage claim
Гитар	Gitar	Guitar
Гов	Gov	Cow
Грамм	Gramm	Gram
Гугирд	Gugird	Matches (matchbox)
Гузашта	Guzashta	Last (previously)
Гузашта	Guzashta	Past (ago)
Гузаштан	Guzashtan	Pass
Гузоштан	Guzoshtan	Put
Гул	Gul	Flower
Гулӯ	Gulu	Throat
Гулобӣ	Gulobi	Pink
Гулхан	Gulkhan	Campfire
Гум кардан	Gum kardan	Lose
Гумрук	Gumruk	Customs
Гумшуда	Gumshuda	Lost
Гунаҳкор	Gunahkor	Guilty
Гунг	Gung	Mute
Гурба	Gurba	Cat
Гурусна	Gurusna	Hungry (famished)
Гуруҳ	Guruh	Band (musician)
Гурӯҳ	Guruh	Team
Гуфтан	Guftan	Say
Гуфтан	Guftan	Tell
Гуфтугӯ кардан	Guftugu kardan	Chat up
Гуш	Gush	Ear
Гушт	Gusht	Meat
Гушти гов	Gushti gov	Beef
Гушти хук	Gushti khuk	Pork
Гӯш кардан	Gush kardan	Listen

Tajik	Pronunciation	English

Ғ

Ғайриимконпазир	Ghayriimkonpazir	Impossible
Ғайриоддӣ	Ghayrioddi	Unusual
Ғалладона	Ghalladona	Cereal
Ғарб	Gharb	West
Ғафс	Ghafs	Thick
Ғизо	Ghizo	Food
Ғолиб	Gholib	Winner
Ғӯтазанӣ	Ghutazani	Diving
Ғуруби офтоб	Ghurubi oftob	Sunset

Д

Давидан	Davidan	Jogging
Давидан	Davidan	Run
Давидан	Davidan	Running
Давра	Davra	Cycle
Дақиқа	Daqiqa	Minute (moment)
Дандон	Dandon	Teeth
Дандон	Dandon	Tooth
Дандонпизишк	Dandonpizishk	Dentist
Дар	Dar	At
Дар	Dar	Door
Дар	Dar	Road
Дар байни	Dar bayni	Between
Дар бари	Dar bari	Beside
Дар болои	Dar boloi	Above
Дар даруни	Dar daruni	In
Дар дохили	Dar dokhili	Aboard
Дар куҷо	Dar kujo	Where
Дар назди	Dar nazdi	In front of
Дар назди	Dar nazdi	Next to
Дар онҷо	Dar onjo	There
Дар поён	Dar poyon	Below

82

Tajik	Pronunciation	English
Дар чорчӯбаи	Dar chorchubai	Within (until)
Дарахт	Darakht	Tree
Дараҷа	Daraja	Degrees (weather)
Дарвоза	Darvoza	Departure gate
Дарвоза	Darvoza	Gate (airport)
Даргирондан	Dargironda	On
Дард	Dard	Pain
Дард	Dard	Sore
Дарди меъда	Dardi me'da	Stomach ache
Дарднок	Dardnok	Painful
Дарё	Daryo	River
Даридан	Daridan	Rip-off
Дароз	Daroz	Long
Даромадан	Daromadan	Enter
Дарун	Darun	Inside
Даст	Dast	Arm
Даст	Dast	Hand
Дастархон	Dastarkhon	Tablecloth
Дасткашак	Dastkashak	Gloves
Дастпоккунак	Dastpokkunak	Napkin
Дафтар	Daftar	Notebook
Даҳон	Dahon	Mouth
Даҳшатангез	Dahshatangez	Awful
Даъват кардан	Da'vat kardan	Invite
Девона	Devona	Crazy
Дегча	Degcha	Saucepan
Дезодорант	Dezodorant	Deodorant
Дер кардан	Der kardan	Delay
Деҳа	Deha	Village
Дигар	Digar	Another
Дигар	Digar	Other
Дидан	Didan	See
Дил	Dil	Heart
Дилбеҳузурӣ	Dilbehuzuri	Nausea
Дилгир	Dilgir	Bored
Дилгиркунанда	Dilgirkunanda	Boring

Tajik	Pronunciation	English
Дин	Din	Religion
Динӣ	Dini	Religious
Дирӯз	Diruz	Yesterday
Дод задан	Dod zadan	Shout
Додан	Dodan	Give
Дока	Doka	Gauze
Донача	Donacha	Rash
Донистан	Donistan	Know
Донишчӯ	Donishju	Student
Дору	Doru	Medicine (medicinals)
Дору	Doru	Pill
Доруқуттӣ	Doruqutti	First-aid kit
Дорухат	Dorukhat	Prescription
Дорухона	Dorukhona	Pharmacy
Дохил	Dokhil	Included
Дохили бино	Dokhili bino	Indoor
Доштан	Doshtan	Have
Доя	Doya	Babysitter
Дӯст	Dust	Date (companion)
Дӯст доштан	Dust doshtan	Like
Дӯст доштан	Dust doshtan	Love
Ду	Du	Two
Ду карата	Du karata	Twice
Ду хучрага	Du hujraga	Double room
Дубора истифода бурдан	Dubora istifoda burdan	Recycle
Дугона	Dugona	Girlfriend
Дугоник	Dugonik	Twins
Дуздӣ	Duzdi	Robbery
Дузд	Duzd	Thief
Дуздидан	Duzdidan	Rob
Дуздидан	Duzdidan	Steal
Дуздидашуда	Duzdidashuda	Stolen
Дуо	Duo	Prayer
Дур	Dar	Far
Дурӯғ гуфтан	Durugh guftan	Lie (falsehood)

Tajik	Pronunciation	English
Дурӯғгу	Durughgu	Liar
Дурдаст	Durdast	Remote
Дуредгар	Duredgar	Carpenter
Дуто	Duto	Double
Духтар	Dukhtar	Daughter
Духтар	Dukhtar	Girl
Духтур	Dukhtur	Doctor
Душ	Dush	Shower
Душвор	Dushvor	Difficult
Дуюм	Duyum	Second
Дӯхтан	Dukhtan	Sew

Ё

Ё	Yo	Or
Евро	Yevro	Euro
Ёзондан	Yozondan	Sprain
Ёри додан	Yori dodan	Help

З

Забон	Zabon	Language
Замин	Zamin	Land
Зан	Zan	Female
Зан	Zan	Wife
Занг задан	Zang zadan	Call (telephone call)
Занг задан	Zang zadan	Ring (ringing)
Занҷирак	Zanjirak	Zipper
Зарар расондан	Zarar rasondan	Hurt
Зард	Zard	Yellow
Зарурат	Zarurat	Necessity
Зарф	Zarf	Jar
Захмбанд	Zakhmband	Bandage
Захмбанди часпак (лейкопластырь)	Zakhmbandi chaspak (leykoplastyr')	Band-Aid
Заҳрнок	Zahrnok	Poisonous

Tajik	Pronunciation	English
Зебо	Zebo	Beautiful
Зебо	Zebo	Handsome
Зебо	Zebo	Pretty
Зиёд шудан	Ziyod shudan	Grow
Зиқ	Ziq	Sad
Зимистон	Zimiston	Winter
Зиндагӣ	Zindagi	Life
Зиндагӣ кардан	Zindagi kardan	Live (occupy)
Зиндон	Zindon	Jail
Зич	Zich	Tight
Зодрӯз	Zodruz	Birthday
Зону	Zonu	Knee
Зуд-зуд	Zud-zud	Often
Зудшикан	Zudshikan	Fragile

И

Ид	Id	Holiday
Идора	Idora	Office
Идораи пулис	Idorai pulis	Police station
Идхо	Idho	Holidays
Издивоҷ	Izdivoj	Marriage
Издивоҷ кардан	Izdivoj kardan	Marry
Иқбол	Iqbol	Luck
Илм	Ilm	Science
Имзо	Imzo	Signature
Имзо кардан	Imzo kardan	Sign (signature)
Имзои ситора	Imzoi sitora	Star sign
Имконпазир	Imkonpazir	Possible
Имрӯз	Imruz	Today
Имшаб	Imshab	Tonight
Ин	In	This (one)
Интизор будан	Intizor budam	Wait
Интиқол дода	Intiqol doda	Transport
Интихоб кардан	Intihob kardan	Choose
Инҷо	Injo	Here

Tajik	Pronunciation	English
Истгоҳ	Istgoh	Station
Истгоҳ	Istgoh	Stop (station)
Истгоҳи автобусҳо	Istgohi avtobusho	Bus station
Истгоҳи автобусҳо	Istgohi avtobusho	Bus stop
Истгоҳи роҳи оҳан	Istgohi rohi ohan	Train station
Истеҳсол кардан	Istehsol kardan	Produce
Истироҳат кардан	Istirohat kardan	Relax
Истодан	Istodan	Stay (sleepover)
Истодан	Istodan	Stop (halt)
Исфаноҷ	Isfanoj	Spinach
Итмом	Itmom	Finish
Ифлос	Iflos	Dirty
Ифлоскунӣ	Ifloskuni	Pollution
Иҷозат	Ijozat	Permission (permit)
Иҷора	Ijora	Rent
Иҷора гирифтан	Ijora giriftan	Hire
Иҷро	Ijro	Performance

К

Кӣ	Ki	Who
Қабл аз	Qabl az	Before
Қабр	Qabr	Grave
Қабристон	Qabriston	Cemetery
Кабуди беранг	Kabudi berang	Blue (light blue)
Кабуди серранг	Kabudi serrang	Blue (dark blue)
Қабул кардан	Qabul kardan	Admit
Қабурға	Qaburgha	Rib
Кабутар	Kabutar	Pigeon
Қадам	Qadam	Step
Қадима	Qadima	Antique
Кадом	Kadom	Which
Каду	Kadu	Pumpkin
Кадуи сабз	Kadui sabz	Zucchini
Қаиқи муҳаррикдор	Qaiqi muharrikdor	Motorboat
Кай	Kay	When

Tajik	Pronunciation	English
Қаймоқ	Qaymoq	Cream (creamy)
Қайчй	Qaychi	Scissors
Қалам	Qalam	Pen
Қалам	Qalam	Pencil
Каламуш	Kalamush	Rat
Қаланфур	Qalanfur	Pepper (peppery)
Калид	Kalid	Key
Калима	Kalima	Word
Калисои чомеъ	Kalisoi jome	Cathedral
Калон	Kalon	Big
Калон	Kalon	Large
Қалъа	Qal'a	Castle
Кам	Kam	Little (few)
Камбағал	Kambaghal	Poor
Камбизоатй	Kambizoati	Poverty
Камбудй	Kambudi	Shortage
Камтар	Kamtar	Less
Қанд	Qand	Candy
Кар	Kar	Deaf
Карам	Karam	Lettuce
Кардан	Kardan	Do
Кардан	Kardan	Make
Қарз	Qarz	Credit
Қарз гирифтан	Qarz giriftan	Borrow
Қарор додан	Qaror dodan	Decide
Картошка	Kartoshka	Potato
Касал	Kasal	Sick
Касалии бахр	Kasalii bahr	Seasickness
Касб кардан	Kasb kardan	Earn
Касе	Kase	Someone
Кат	Kat	Bed
Кати дукаса	Kati dukasa	Double bed
Қатор	Qator	Queue
Қаттора	Qattora	Train
Қафаси сина	Qafasi sina	Chest (torso)
Кафолат дода	Kafolat doda	Guaranteed

Tajik	Pronunciation	English
мешавад	meshavad	
Қаҳва	Qahva	Coffee
Қаҳваранг	Qahvarang	Brown
Кашидн	Kashidn	Pull
Кӯдак	Kudak	Baby
Кӯдак	Kudak	Child
Кӯдакон	Kudakon	Children
Килограмм	Kilogram	Kilogram
Километр	Kilometr	Kilometer
Қимат	Qimat	Expensive
Қисм	Qism	Part (piece)
Қисм	Qism	Piece
Кисса	Kissa	Pocket
Китоб	Kitob	Book
Китоби телефон	Kitobi telefon	Phone book
Китобхона	Kitobkhona	Library
Китф	Kitf	Shoulder
Киштй	Kishti	Ship
Клавиатура	Klaviatura	Keyboard
Клуб	Klub	Nightclub
Қоғаз	Qoghaz	Paper
Қоғази ташноб	Qoghazi tashnob	Toilet paper
Қоғази тунук	Qoghazi tunuk	Tissues
Қоғази хатнависй	Qoghazi khatnavisi	Postcard
Қоида	Qoida	Rule
Қолин	Qolin	Rug
Коллеҷ	Kollej	College
Компютер	Kompyuter	Computer
Кондитсионер	Konditsioner	Air conditioning
Кондитсионер	Konditsioner	Conditioner (conditioning treatment)
Консерт	Konsert	Concert
Қонун	Qonun	Law (edict)
Қонуншиканй	Qonunshikani	Foul
Кор	Kor	Job

Tajik	Pronunciation	English
Кор	Kor	Operation (process)
Кор	Kor	Work
Корд	Kord	Knife
Кори қоғазй	Kori qoghazi	Paperwork
Коса	Kosa	Bowl
Коса	Kosa	Dish
Костюм барои оббозй	Kostyum baroi obbozi	Bathing suit
Кофй	Kofi	Enough
Кофтан	Koftan	Look for
Қошуқ	Qoshuq	Spoon
Қошуқ	Qoshuq	Teaspoon
Крем	Krem	Sun block
Крем барои тарошидан	Krem baroi taroshidan	Shaving cream
Кӯтал	Kutal	Uphill
Кӯтоҳ	Kutoh	Short (low)
Қувват	Quvvat	Power
Кул	Kul	Lake
Кулоҳ	Kuloh	Hat
Қулф	Qulf	Lock
Қулф	Qulf	Padlock
Қулф кардашуда	Qulf kardashuda	Locked
Қуммаки об	Qummaki ob	Tap water
Кур	Kur	Blind
Курпа	Kurpa	Blanket
Курпача	Kurpacha	Mattress
Курсй	Kursi	Chair
Курта	Kurta	Dress
Курта	Kurta	Shirt
Қуттй	Qutti	Box
Қуттй	Qutti	Can (aluminium can)
Қуттй	Qutti	Tin (aluminium can)
Қуттии об	Quttii ob	Water bottle
Қуттии партовхо	Quttii partovho	Garbage can
Қуттии почта	Quttii pochta	Mailbox
Кух	Kuh	Mountain

Tajik	Pronunciation	English
Куҳна	Kuhna	Ancient
Куҳна	Kuhna	Old
Кушод	Kushod	Wide
Кушодан	Kushodan	Open
Кушояндаи шиша	Kushoyandai shisha	Bottle opener (beer)
Кушояндаи шиша	Kushoyandai shisha	Bottle opener (corkscrew)
Куштор	Kushtor	Murder
Кӯча	Kucha	Street
Кӯшиш кардан	Kushish kardan	Try (trying)

Л

Лабсурхкунак	Labsurkhkunak	Lipstick
Лабҳо	Labho	Lips
Лагер	Lager	Camp
Лақаб	Laqab	Nickname
Ламс кардан	Lams kardan	Touch
Лезбианка	Lezbianka	Lesbian
Лекин	Lekin	But
Лептоп	Leptop	Laptop
Либос	Libos	Clothing
Либоси оббозй	Libosi obbozi	Swimsuit
Лимонад	Limonad	Lemonade
Лиму	Limu	Lemon
Линзаҳо	Linzaho	Contact lenses
Линзаҳо	Linzaho	Lens
Лифт	Lift	Elevator
Лой	Loy	Mud

М

Мавсим	Mavsim	Season
Мавҷ	Mavj	Wave
Магас	Magas	Mosquito
Мағоза	Maghoza	Shop

91

Tajik	Pronunciation	English
Мағоза	Maghoza	Shop
Мағозаи китоб	Maghozai kitob	Bookshop
Мағозаи машрубот	Maghozai mashrubot	Liquor store
Мағозаи хӯрока	Maghozai khuroka	Grocery
Май	May	Wine
Майда	Mayda	Change (coinage)
Майда	Mayda	Change (pocket change)
Майдон	Maydon	Square (town center)
Майхона	Maykhona	Pub
Макон	Makon	Venue
Мактаб	Maktab	School
Мактаби олй	Maktabi oli	High school
Мактуб	Maktub	Letter (envelope)
Малика	Malika	Queen
Ман	Man	Me
Манах	Manah	Jaw
Манфй	Manfi	Negative
Манъ кардан	Man' kardan	Stop (avoid)
Маориф	Maorif	Education
Марказ	Markaz	Center
Маркази савдо	Markazi savdo	Shopping center
Маркази шахр	Markazi shahr	City center
Маршрут	Marshrut	Route
Маст	Mast	Drunk
Матои шӯстанй	Matoi shustani	Wash cloth
Махаллй	Mahalli	Local
Махбас	Mahbas	Prison
Махсулоти кӯлолгарй	Mahsuloti kulolgari	Pottery
Мачалла	Majalla	Magazine
Машхур	Mashhur	Famous
Машхур	Mashhur	Popular
Маълумот	Ma'lumot	Information
Маънодор	Ma'nodor	Sensible
Маъюб	Ma'yub	Disabled
Мебел	Mebel	Furniture

Tajik	Pronunciation	English
Мева	Meva	Fruit
Метал	Metal	Metal
Метр	Metr	Meter
Метро	Metro	Subway (underground)
Меҳмонхона	Mehmonkhona	Hotel
Меҳмонхона	Mehmonkhona	Motel
Меҳрубон	Mehrubon	Kind (sweet)
Меъда	Me'da	Stomach
Мӯза	Muza	Boots (shoes)
Микромавҷи	Mikromavji	Microwave
Милиметр	Milimetr	Millimeter
Миннатдор	Minnatdor	Grateful
Мӯй	Muy	Hair
Мӯйгирӣ	Muygiri	Haircut
Мӯйчинак	Muychinak	Tweezers
Мо	Mo	We
Мовар кардан	Mosvar kardan	Trust
Модар	Modar	Mother
Монанд	Monand	Similar
Монда шуда	Monda shuda	Tired
Монда шудан	Monda shudan	Tire
Мор	Mor	Snake
Мотосикл	Motosikl	Motorbike
Моҳӣ	Mohi	Fish
Моҳ	Moh	Month
Мошина	Moshina	Machine
Мошинаи либосшӯй	Moshinai libosshui	Washing machine
Мошини боркаш	Moshini borkash	Truck
Муайянкунӣ	MuayyankunI	Identification
Муаллим	Muallim	Teacher
Музд	Muzd	Wage
Мукаммал	Mukammal	Perfect
Муқобил	Muqobil	Opposite
Мулоқот кардан	Muloqot kardan	Talk
Муносиб	Munosib	Right (appropriate)

Tajik	Pronunciation	English
Муносибат	Munosibat	Relationship
Муосир	Muosir	Modern
Мурғобй	Murghobi	Duck
Мурда	Murda	Dead
Мурдан	Murdan	Die
Мусбат	Musbat	Positive
Мусиқй	Musiqi	Music
Мусобиқа	Musobiqa	Race (running)
Мусофир	Musofir	Passenger
Мутахассис	Mutakhassis	Specialist
Мухим	Muhim	Important
Муҳофизат кардан	Muhofizat kardan	Protect
Муҳр	Muhr	Stamp
Мухталиф	Mukhtalif	Different
Муш	Mush	Mouse
Мушак	Mushak	Muscle

Н

На... на....	Na... na....	Neither...nor...
Набера (духтар)	Nabera (dukhtar)	Granddaughter
Набера (писар)	Nabera (pisar)	Grandson
Нав	Nav	New
Навбатй	Navbati	Next (ensuing)
Навиштан	Navishtan	Write
Навмсанда	Navmsanda	Writer
Навохтан	Navokhtan	Play (strum)
Навъ	Nav'	Type
Назди шаҳр	Nazdi shahr	Suburb
Наздик	Nazdik	Close (closer)
Наздик	Nazdik	Near (close)
Наздиктарин	Nazdiktarin	Nearest
Назм	Nazm	Rhythm
Нақд	Naqd	Cash (deposit a check)
Намак	Namak	Salt

94

Tajik	Pronunciation	English
Намнок	Namnok	Humid
Намоиш	Namoish	View
Нарх	Narkh	Price
Насос	Nasos	Pump
Нафас кашидан	Nafas kashidan	Breathe
Не	Ne	No
Не	Ne	Not
Нигарон	Nigaron	Worried
Нигоҳ кардан	Nigoh kardan	Look
Нимавақт	Nimavaqt	Part-time
Нимбирён	Nimbiryon	Steak
Нисф	Nisf	Half
Нисфи шаб	Nisfi shab	Midnight
Нисфирӯзӣ	Nisfiruzi	Midday
Нисфирӯзӣ	Nisfiruzi	Noon
Нишеб	Nisheb	Steep
Нишон додан	Nishon dodan	Show
Нишон додан	Nishon dodan	Show
Нодир	Nodir	Rare (exotic)
Нодир	Nodir	Rare (unique)
Нодуруст	Nodurust	Wrong
Нок	Nok	Pear
Ноқисулақл	Noqisulaql	Idiot
Ном	Nom	Name (moniker)
Ном	Nom	Name (term)
Ном	Nom	Name (surname)
Нон	Non	Bread
Нонпазхона	Nonpazkhona	Bakery
Нороҳат	Norohat	Uncomfortable
Нохунгирак	Nokhungirak	Nail clippers
Ношинос	Noshinos	Stranger
Нуқра	Nuqra	Silver
Нуқта	Nuqta	Point
Нуқтаи сӯзишворӣ	Nuqtai suzishvori	Petrol station
Нушокии спиртӣ	Nushokii spirti	Alcohol
Нӯшидан	Nushidan	Drink (cocktail)

Tajik	Pronunciation	English
Нӯшидан	Nushidan	Drink (beverage)
Нӯшидан	Nushidan	Drink
Нӯшокӣ	Nushoki	Soft-drink

О

Об	Ob	Water
Оби гарм	Obi garm	Hot water
Оби ҷав	Obi jav	Beer
Обногузар	Obnoguzar	Waterproof
Обу ҳаво	Obu havo	Weather
Овардан	Ovardan	Bring
Овоз	Ovoz	Voice
Овоз додан	Ovoz dodan	Vote
Оғоз	Oghoz	Start
Огоҳ кардан	Ogoh kardan	Warn
Оғӯш кардан	Oghush kardan	Hug
Одам	Odam	Person
Одам, мард	Odam, mard	Man
Одамон	Odamon	People
Оддӣ	Oddi	Ordinary
Оддӣ	Oddi	Typical
Озод	Ozod	Free (at liberty)
Озодмоҳӣ	Ozodmohi	Salmon
Оила	Oila	Family
Оина	Oina	Mirror
Оксиген	Oksigen	Oxygen
Олӣ	Oli	Great (wonderful)
Олим	Olim	Scientist
Олиҷаноб	Olijanob	Wonderful
Олу	Olu	Plum
Омӯхтан	Omukhtan	Learn
Он	On	It
Он	On	That (one)
Онҳо	Onho	They
Оператор	Operator	Operator

Tajik	Pronunciation	English
Орд	Ord	Flour
Орзу	Orzu	Dream
Орзу кардан	Orzu kardan	Wish
Оркестр	Orkestr	Orchestra
Ороиш	Oroish	Make-up
Ором	Orom	Quiet
Осеб	Oseb	Injury
Осмон	Osmon	Sky
Осон	Oson	Easy
Осон	Oson	Simple
Осорхона	Osorkhona	Museum
Оташ	Otash	Fire (heated)
Оташфрӯзак	Otashfruzak	Lighter (ignited)
Офат	Ofat	Disaster
Офтоб	Oftob	Sun
Офтобӣ	Oftobi	Sunny
Оҳак	Ohak	Lime
Охир	Okhir	End
Охири ҳафта	Okhiri hafta	Weekend
Охирон	Okhiron	Last (finale)
Оҳиста	Ohista	Slow
Оҳиста	Ohista	Slowly
Ошёна	Oshona	Floor (level)
Ошхона	Oshkhona	Kitchen
Оянда	Oyanda	Future

П

Пагоҳ	Pagoh	Tomorrow
Падар	Padar	Dad
Паём	Payom	Message
Пайкара	Paykara	Statue
Пайравӣ кардан	Payravi kardan	Follow
Пакет	Paket	Packet
Палто	Palto	Coat
Панир	Panir	Cheese

Tajik	Pronunciation	English
Парвоз кардан	Parvoz kardan	Fly
Пардохт	Pardokht	Payment
Пардохт кардан	Pardokht kardan	Pay
Парк	Park	Park
Парондан	Parondan	Shoot
Парранда	Parranda	Bird
Партов	Partov	Garbage
Парҳез	Parhez	Diet
Пас	Pas	Back (backward position)
Пас	Pas	Behind
Пас	Pas	Rear (behind)
Пасандоз	Pasandoz	Deposit
Паст	Past	Low
Пасткунандаи дард	Pastkunandai dar	Painkiller
Пахта	Pahta	Cotton
Пашм	Pashm	Wool
Педал	Pedal	Pedal
Пеш	Pesh	Ago
Пешво	Peshvo	Leader
Пешпо хӯрдан	Peshpo khurdan	Tip (tipping)
Пешхизмат	Peshkhizmat	Waiter
Пирог	Pirog	Pie
Писар	Pisar	Son
Писарбача	Pisarbacha	Boy
Пластикӣ	Plastiki	Plastic
Подшоҳ	Podshoh	King
Поён	Poyon	Down
Поин	Poin	Bottom (on bottom)
Пой	Poy	Foot
Пой	Poy	Leg
Пойафзол	Poyafzol	Shoes
Поку	Poku	Razor
Помидор	Pomidor	Tomato
Пора	Pora	Bribe
Порт	Port	Port (dock)

Tajik	Pronunciation	English
Порча	Porcha	Lump
Порча	Porcha	Slice
Почта	Pochta	Post office
Президент	Prezident	President
Принтер	Printer	Printer (printing)
Пӯст	Pust	Skin
Пул	Pul	Bridge
Пул	Pul	Money
Пулис	Pulis	Police
Пур кардан	Pur kardan	Fill
Пурра	Purra	Full
Пухтан	Puhtan	Cook
Пушаймон шудан	Pushaymon shudan	Regret
Пушт	Pusht	Back (body)
Пӯшида	Pushida	Closed
Пӯшидан	Pushidan	Close
Пӯшидан	Pushidan	Shut
Пӯшидан	Pushidan	Wear

Р

Tajik	Pronunciation	English
Равған	Ravghan	Oil (oily)
Равшан	Ravshan	Light
Равшан	Ravshan	Light (pale)
Рад кардан	Rad kardan	Refuse
Радиатор	Radiator	Radiator
Радио	Radio	Radio
Рақам	Raqam	Number
Рақами хучра	Raqami hujra	Room number
Ракс	Raqs	Dancing
Ракс кардан	Raqs kardan	Dance
Ранг	Rang	Color
Расид	Rasid	Bill (bill of sale)
Расид	Rasid	Receipt
Расидан	Rasidan	Arrive
Расиданхо	Rasidanxo	Arrivals

Tajik	Pronunciation	English
Расм	Rasm	Painting (canvas)
Расм	Rasm	Painting (the art)
Расонидани	Rasonidani	Deliver
Рассом	Rassom	Painter
Растани	Rastani	Plant
Рафиқ	Rafik	Friend
Рафтан	Raftan	Go (walk)
Рафтан	Raftan	Go (drive)
Рег	Reg	Sand
Рӯз	Ruz	Day
Рӯзи дигар	Ruzi digar	Day after tomorrow
Рӯзи қабл аз дирӯз	Ruzi qabl az diruz	Day before yesterday
Рӯзнома	Ruznoma	Diary
Рӯзнома	Ruznoma	Newspaper
Рӯй	Ruy	Face
Рӯймол	Ruymol	Scarf
Рӯмолча	Rumolcha	Handkerchief
Розй шудан	Rozi shudan	Agree
Ройгон	Roygon	Complimentary (on the house)
Ройгон	Roygon	Free (no cost)
Ром	Rom	Rum
Романтикй	Romantiki	Romantic
Рондан	Rondan	Drive
Рондан	Rondan	Ride
Рондан	Rondan	Ride (riding)
Рост	Rost	Direct
Рост	Rost	Right (rightward)
Рост	Rost	Straight
Роҳ	Roh	Path
Роҳ	Roh	Way
Роҳ гаштан	Roh gashtan	Walk
Роҳат кардан	Rohat kardan	Rest
Роҳгузар	Rohguzar	Pedestrian
Роҳи асосй	Rohi asosi	Mainroad
Роҳкиро	Rohkiro	Fare

Tajik	Pronunciation	English
Роҳрав	Rohrav	Track (pathway)
Руҳонй	Ruhoni	Priest

С

Tajik	Pronunciation	English
Сабаб	Sabab	Reason
Сабад	Sabad	Basket
Сабз	Sabz	Green
Сабзавот	Sabzavot	Vegetable
Сабт кардан	Sabt kardan	Record (music)
Сабук	Sabuk	Light (weightless)
Савдо	Savdo	Sale (special)
Савдо	Savdo	Trade (trading)
Савдо	Savdo	Trade (career)
Савол	Savol	Question
Савол додан	Savol dodan	Ask (questinoning)
Савор шудан	Savor shudan	Board (climb aboard)
Саг	Sag	Dog
Саёҳат кардан	Sayohat kardan	Hike
Саёҳат кардан	Sayohat kardan	Hiking
Саёҳат кардан	Sayohat kardan	Tour
Сайёра	Sayyora	Planet
Сайёҳ	Sayyoh	Tourist
Сайр кардан	Sayr kardan	Trip (expedition)
Салат	Salat	Salad
Саломатй	Salomati	Health
Самт	Samt	Direction
Сана	Sana	Date (important notice)
Сана	Sana	Date (specific day)
Санг	Sang	Stone
Санобар	Sanobar	Sexy
Сантиметр	Santimetr	Centimeter
Санъат	San"at	Art
Сар	Sar	Head
Сарватманд	Sarvatmand	Wealthy

Tajik	Pronunciation	English
Сардард	Sardard	Headache
Саривақт	Sarivaqt	On time
Сармо	Sarmo	Frost
Сароидан	Saroidan	Sing
Саросема будан	Sarosema budan	(be) in a hurry
Сарошпаз	Saroshpaz	Chef
Сароянда	Saroyanda	Singer
Сарҳад	Sarhad	Border
Сатр	Satr	String
Сауна	Sauna	Sauna
Сафар кардан	Safar kardan	Travel
Сафед	Safed	White
Саҳар	Sahar	Morning
Саҳифа	Sahifa	Page
Сахт	Sakht	Hard (firm)
Сахт чӯшондашуда	Sakht jushondashuda	Hard-boiled
Сачоқ	Sachoq	Towel
Светофор	Svetofor	Traffic light
Свитер	Sviter	Sweater
Себ	Seb	Apple
Сент	Sent	Cent
Серғавғо	Serghavgho	Noisy
Серфинг кардан	Serfing kardan	Surf
Сеюм	Seyum	Third
Сӯзан	Suzan	Needle (stitch)
Сӯзишворӣ	Suzishvori	Gas (gasoline)
Сӯзишворӣ	Sūzishvori	Petrol
Сигар	Sigar	Cigar
Сигарет	Sigaret	Cigarette
Сиёсат	Siyosat	Politics
Сиёҳ	Siyoh	Black
Силсилакӯҳ	Silsilakuh	Mountain range
Синабанд	Sinaband	Bra
Синамо	Sinamo	Movie
Синну сол	Sinnu sol	Age
Синф	Sinf	Class (categorize)

Tajik	Pronunciation	English
Сирко	Sirko	Vinegar
Ситора	Sitora	Star
Сифат	Sifat	Quality
Соат	Soat	Clock
Соат	Soat	Hour
Соат	Soat	Watch
Соати зангдор	Soati zangdor	Alarm clock
Собун	Sobun	Soap
Сода	Soda	Soda
Сол	Sol	Year
Солхо	Solho	Years
Сония	Soniya	Second (moment)
Соус	Sous	Sauce
Соҳиб	Sohib	Owner
Соҳил	Sohil	Beach
Соҳил	Sohil	Coast
Сохти дастӣ	Sokhti dasti	Handmade
Соя	Soya	Shade (shady)
Студио	Studio	Studio
Субҳ	Subh	Dawn
Сулфидан	Sulfidan	Cough
Сулҳ	Sulh	Peace
Сумка	Sumka	Bag
Сумка	Sumka	Handbag
Супермаркет	Supermarket	Supermarket
Сурат	Surat	Photo
Сурат гирифтан	Surat giriftan	Take photos
Суратгир	Suratgir	Photographer
Сурин	Surin	Bottom (butt)
Суроға	Surogha	Address
Суруд	Surud	Song
Сурх	Surkh	Red
Суръат	Sur'at	Speed (rate)
Сӯхта	Sukhta	Sunburn
Сюрприз	Syurpriz	Surprise

103

Tajik	Pronunciation	English

Т

Tajik	Pronunciation	English
Таб	Tab	Fever
Табақ	Tabaq	Plate
Табассум	Tabassum	Smile
Табиат	Tabiat	Nature
Таваққуф кардан	Tavaquf kardan	Park (parking)
Тавонистан	Tavonistan	Can (have the ability)
Тавсия	Tavsiya	Advice
Тавсия	Tavsiya	Recomment
Тағйирот	Taghyirot	Change
Тагпӯш	Tagpush	Underwear
Тайёр	Tayyor	Ready
Тайёр кардан	Tayyor kardan	Prepare
Тайёра	Tayyora	Airplane
Тайёра	Tayyora	Plane
Таксарй	Taksari	Pillow
Тақсим кардан	Taqsim kardan	Deal (card dealer)
Тақсим кардан	Taqsim kardan	Share (sharing)
Тақсим кардан	Taqsim kardan	Share (allotment)
Талони саворшавй	Taloni savorshavi	Boarding pass
Талх	Talkh	Bitter
Тамашк	Tamashk	Raspberry
Тамоку	Tamoku	Tobacco
Тамоку кашидан	Tamoku kashidan	Smoke
Тамоку намекашида	Tamoku namekashida	Nonsmoking
Тамошо кардан	Tamosho kardan	Watch
Танбал	Tanbal	Lazy
Танӯр	Tanur	Oven
Танур	Tanur	Stove
Танхо	Tanho	Alone
Танхо	Tanho	Only
Танхо	Tanxo	Single (individual)
Таоми шом	Taomi shom	Dinner
Таппонча	Tapponcha	Gun

Tajik	Pronunciation	English
Тар	Tar	Wet
Тарабхона	Tarabkhona	Restaurant
Тараф	Taraf	Side
Тарк	Tark	Departure
Тарк кардан	Tark kardan	Depart
Тарк кардан	Tark kardan	Quit
Таркиб	Tarkib	Ingredient
Тарошидан	Taroshidan	Shave
Тарсидан	Tarsidan	Afraid
Тартиб	Tartib	Order
Тару тоза	Taru toza	Fresh
Тарчума	Tarjuma	Translation
Тарчума кардан	Tarjuma kardan	Translate
Тасмаи бехатарӣ	Tasmai bekhatari	Seatbelt
Тафсилот	Tafsilot	Details
Тахмин кардан	Takhmin kardan	Guess
Тахта	Takhta	Wood
Тачриба	Tajriba	Experience
Ташаккур кардан	Tashakkur kardan	Thank
Ташна	Tashna	Thirsty (parched)
Ташриф	Tashrif	Visit
Ташриф овардан	Tashrif ovardan	Visit
Таъкиб кардан	Ta'qib kardan	Track (racing)
Таъмир	Ta'mir	Repair
Таърих	Ta'rikh	History
Таътил	Ta'til	Vacation
Тӯб	Tub	Ball (sports)
ТВ	TV	TV
Театр	Teatr	Theater
Тез	Tez	Fast
Тез	Tez	Quick
Тезпазонак	Tezpazonak	Frying pan
Тела додан	Tela dodan	Push
Телевизор	Televizor	Television
Телефон	Telefon	Telephone
Телефони мобилӣ	Telefoni mobili	Cell phone

Tajik	Pronunciation	English
Телефони мобилй	Telefoni mobili	Mobile phone
Теппа	Teppa	Hill
Тилло	Tillo	Gold
Тирамох	Tiramoh	Fall (autumnal)
Тиреза	Tireza	Window
Тӯй	Tuy	Wedding
То	To	Until
Тоба	Toba	Pan
Тобистон	Tobiston	Summer
Тоза	Toza	Clean
Тоза	Toza	Pure
Тозакунй	Tozakuni	Cleaning
Толори варзишй	Tolori varzishi	Gym
Торик	Torik	Dark
Тоскулох	Toskuloh	Helmet
Тост	Tost	Toast (toasting)
Тостер	Toster	Toaster
Трамвай	Tramvay	Tram
Ту	Tu	You
Тулӯи офтоб	Tului oftob	Sunrise
Тумандор	Tumandor	Foggy
Тунук	Tunuk	Thin
Тур	Tur	Net
Туркия	Turkiya	Turkey
Тути заминй	Tuti zamini	Strawberry
Тухм	Tukhm	Egg
Тухфа	Tuhfa	Gift
Тухфа	Tuhfa	Present (treat)

У

Узв	Uzv	Member
Укёнус	Uqyonus	Ocean
Универмаг	Univermag	Department store
Уребча	Urebcha	Diaper
Урф	Urf	Custom

Tajik	Pronunciation	English

Ф

Tajik	Pronunciation	English
Фаврй	Favri	Urgent
Фарбеҳ	Farbeh	Fat
Фарёд кардан	Faryod kardan	Call
Фарқияти вақт	Farqiyati vaqt	Time difference
Фармон	Farmon	Order
Фаромадан	Faromadan	Get off (disembark)
Фаромуш кардан	Faromush kardan	Forget
Фарш	Farsh	Floor (carpeting)
Фаҳмидан	Fahmidan	Understand
Фаъолият	Fa'oliyat,	Business
Ферма	Ferma	Farm
Фикр кардан	Fikr kardan	Think
Фиреб кардан	Fireb kardan	Cheat
Фиристондан	Firistondan	Send
Фишор	Fishor	Pressure
Фоида	Foida	Profit
Фоидаовар	Foidaovar	Useful
Фоиз	Foiz	Per cent
Фойтун	Foytun	Carriage
Фунт	Funt	Pound (ounces)
Фурӯзонак	Furūzonak	Light bulb
Фурориш	Furorish	Downhill
Фурудгоҳ	Furudgoh	Airport
Фурӯхтан	Furukhtan	Sell
Футболка	Futbolka	T-shirt

Ҳ

Tajik	Pronunciation	English
Ҳа	Ha	Yes
Хабарнав	Khabarnav	News
Ҳабс кардан	Ҳabs kardan	Arrest
Ҳавз	Havz	Pool (basin)
Ҳавз	Havz	Swiming pool

Tajik	Pronunciation	English
Ҳаво	Havo	Air
Хазиначӣ	Hazinachi	Cashier
Ҳайвон	Hayvon	Animal
Ҳалқа	Halqa	Ring (bauble)
Ҳам	Ham	Also
Ҳам	Ham	Too (additionally)
Ҳама	Hama	All
Ҳамеша	Hamesha	Always
Ҳамеша	Hamesha	Forever
Хамираи дандоншӯй	Khamirai dandonshui	Toothpaste
Ҳамом	Hamom	Bath
Ҳамом	Hamom	Bathroom
Ҳамшира	Hamshira	Nurse
Хандовар	Khandovar	Funny
Ҳанӯз	Hanuz	(Not) yet
Ҳар як	Har yak	Each
Ҳар як	Har yak	Every
Ҳар як	Har yak	Per
Ҳар як кас	Har yak kas	Everyone
Ҳар як чиз	Har yak chiz	Everything
Ҳаракат	Harakat	Traffic
Ҳарбӣ	Harbi	Military
Харбӯза	Kharbuza	Watermelon
Харгӯш	Khargush	Rabbit
Хардал	Khardal	Mustard
Ҳарду	Hardu	Both
Харита	Kharita	Map
Харобаҳо	Kharobaho	Ruins
Ҳарорат	Harorat	Temperature (feverish)
Ҳарорат	Harorat	Temperature (degrees)
Ҳароратсанҷ	Haroratsanj	Thermometer
Ҳаррӯза	Harruza	Daily
Харсанг	Kharsang	Rock
Хатарнок	Khatarnok	Dangerous

Tajik	Pronunciation	English
Хати ҳавой	Khati havoi	Airline
Хато	Khato	Mistake
Хафта	Khafta	Week
Хашмгин	Khashmgin	Angry
Хеле	Khele	Too (excessively)
Хеле	Khele	Very
Ҳеҷ кадом	Hej kadom	None
Ҳеҷ чиз	Hej chiz	Nothing
Ҳеҷгоҳ	Hejgoh	Never
Ҳизб	Hizb	Party (political)
Хизмат	Khizmat	Service
Ҳикоя	Hikoya	Story
Ҳис кардан	His kardan	Feel (touching)
Ҳисоб	Hisob	Account
Ҳисоб кардан	Hisob kardan	Count
Ҳисоби бонкй	Hisobi bonki	Bank account
Ҳиссй	Hissi	Sensual
Ҳиссиёт	Hissiyot	Feelings
Хиҷолат кашида	Khijolat kashida	Embarrassed
Хоб кардан	Khob kardan	Sleep
Хобидан	Khobidan	Lie (lying)
Хоболул	Khobolul	Sleepy
Ҳодиса	Hodisa	Accident
Ҳозир	Hozir	Now
Ҳозир	Hozir	Present (now)
Хока	Khoka	Powder
Хокистарранг	Khokistarang	Grey
Холй	Kholi	Empty
Ҳолатҳои фавқулодда	Holathoi favqulodda	Emergency
Хом	Khoum	Raw
Ҳомиладор	Homilador	Pregnant
Хомӯш	Khomush	Off (strange)
Хона	Khona	Apartment
Хона	Khona	Flat
Хона	Khona	Home
Хона	Khona	House

Tajik	Pronunciation	English
Хондан	Khondan	Read
Хондан	Khondan	Reading
Хонум	Khonum	Miss (lady)
Хонум	Khonum	Mrs./Ms
Хоридан	Khoridan	Itch
Хориҷа	Khorija	Overseas
Хостан	Khostan	Prefer
Хостан	Khostan	Want
Хоҳар	Khohar	Sister
Хоҳиш кардан	Khoχish kardan	Ask (request)
Ҳоҷатхона	Hojatkhona	Public toilet
Ҳоҷатхона	Hojatkhona	Toilet
Ҳоҷҷат	Hojjat	Need
Хӯрдан	Khurdan	Eat
Хӯриш	Khurish	Snack
Хӯрок	Khurok	Meal
Хӯроки нисфирӯзӣ	Khuroki nisfiruzi	Lunch
Хӯроки саҳар	Khuroki sahar	Breakfast
Хуб	Khub	Fine
Хуб	Khub	Good
Хуб	Khub	Nice
Худо	Khudo	God (deity)
Худписанд	Khudpisand	Selfish
Хук	Khuk	Pig
Ҳуқуқӣ	Huquqi	Legal
Ҳукумат	Hukumat	Government
Хун	Khun	Blood
Ҳунар	Hunar	Crafts
Ҳунарманд	χunarmand	Artist
Хурд	Khurd	Little (tiny)
Хурд	Khurd	Small
Хурд	Khurd	Tiny
Хурсандӣ	Khursandi	Fun
Хурсанд	Khursand	Happy
Хурсандӣ кардан	Khursandi kardan	Have fun
Хусусӣ	Khususi	Private

Tajik	Pronunciation	English
Ҳуҷра	Hujra	Room (accommodation)
Ҳуҷра	Hujra	Room (chamber)
Ҳуҷраи интизорӣ	Hujrai intizori	Waiting room
Ҳуҷраи либос ивазкунӣ	Hujrai libos ivazkuni	Changin room
Ҳуҷҷати тасдиқкунанадаи шахсият	Hujjati tasdiqkunanadai shakhsiyat	ID card
Хушбахт	Khushbakht	Lucky
Хушбӯй	Khushbuy	Perfume
Хушдоман	Khushdoman	Mother-in-law
Хушк	Khushk	Dry
Хушк кардан	Khushk kardan	Dry (warm up)
Хӯш омадед	Khush omaded	Welcome

Ч

Чӣ	Chi	What
Чӣ қадар	Chi qadar	How much
Чӣ тавр	Chi tavr	How
Ҷавоб	Javob	Answer
Ҷавон	Javon	Young
Ҷавоҳирот	Javohirot	Jewelry
Ҷадвал	Jadval	Table
Ҷазира	Jazira	Island
Ҷанг	Jang	War
Ҷанг кардан	Jang kardan	Fight
Ҷангал	Jangal	Forest
Чангол	Changol	Fork
Ҷаноб	Janob	Mr.
Ҷануб	Janub	South
Чап	Chap	Left (leftward)
Чарм	Charm	Leather
Чароғҳои пеш	Charoghhoi pesh	Headlights
Чарх	Charkh	Wheel

111

Tajik	Pronunciation	English
Чархзании сар	Charkhzanii sar	Dizzy
Ҷасур	Jasur	Brave
Ҷаҳон	Jahon	World
Чашидан	Chashidan	Try (sip)
Чашмҳо	Chashmho	Eyes
Ҷашн	Jashn	Celebration
Ҷевони либос	Jevoni libos	Wardrobe
Чемпер	Jemper	Jumper (cardigan)
Ҷиддй	Jiddi	Serious
Чизе	Chize	Something
Чизи азизу гаронбахо	Chizi azizu garonbaho	Relic
Чилди таксарй	Jildi taksari	Pillowcase
Ҷинс	Jins	Sex
Ҷинсй	Jinsi	Sexism
Ҷип	Jip	Jeep
Чипта	Chipta	Ticket
Чодир	Chodir	Sheet (linens)
Ҷои гузар	Joi guzar	Aisle
Ҷои нишаст	Joi nishast	Seat
Ҷои хоб	Joi khob	Bedroom
Чой	Choy	Tea
Ҷой	Joy	Place
Чойник	Choynik	Pot (kettle)
Ҷомадон	Jomadon	Suitcase
Чормағз	Chormaghz	Nut
Чоряк	Chiryak	Quarter
Чоҳ	Choh	Well
Ҷӯраб	Jurab	Socks
Чӯткаи дандоншӯй	Chutkai dandonshui	Toothbrush
Ҷуброн кардан	Jubron kardan	Refund
Ҷувздон	Juvzdon	Purse
Ҷуворй	Juvori	Corn
Ҷудо кардан	Judo kardan	Seperate
Чукур	Chuqur	Deep
Чуммак	Jummak	Tap
Чуфт	Juft	Pair

112

Tajik	Pronunciation	English
Чӯҷа	Chuja	Chicken

Ш

Tajik	Pronunciation	English
Шаб	Shab	Night
Шабнишинӣ	Shabnishini	Party (celebration)
Шабонарӯз	Shabonaruz	Overnight
Шавҳар	Shavhar	Husband
Шакар	Shakar	Sugar
Шакл	Shakl	Shape
Шамол	Shamol	Storm
Шамол	Shamol	Wind
Шамол хӯрдан	Shamol khurdan	Have a cold
Шампун	Shampun	Shampoo
Шамсия	Shamsiya	Umbrella
Шамъ	Sham'	Candle
Шапалак	Shapalak	Butterfly
Шарбат	Sharbat	Juice
Шарқ	Sharq	East
Шармгин	Sharmgin	Shy
Шароби себ	Sharobi seb	Cider
Шарт бастан	Shart bastan	Bet
Шартнома	Shartnoma	Contract
Шафтолу	Shaftolu	Peach
Шаҳр	Shahr	City
Шикамрав	Shikamrav	Diarrhea
Шикастагӣ	Shikastagi	Broken (breaking)
Шикоят кардан	Shikoyat kardan	Complain
Шим	Shim	Pants (slacks)
Шимол	Shimol	North
Шино кардан	Shino kardan	Swim
Шинокунӣ	Shinokuni	Cruise
Шиноснома	Shinosnoma	Passport
Шиппак	Shippak	Sandal
Шир	Shir	Milk
Ширеш	Shiresh	Glue

Tajik	Pronunciation	English
Ширинй	Shirini	Dessert
Ширин	Shirin	Sweet
Шиша	Shisha	Bottle
Шиша	Shisha	Glass
Шиштан	Shishtan	Sit
Шоколад	Shokolad	Chocolate
Шона	Shona	Comb
Шона	Shona	Hairbrush
Шонс	Shons	Chance
Шортик	Shortik	Shorts
Шохрох	Shohroh	Highway
Шояд	Shoyad	Maybe
Шӯстан	Shustan	Wash (bathe)
Шӯстан	Shustan	Wash (scrub)
Шукух	Shukuh	Luxury
Шумо	Shumo	You
Шунидан	Shunidan	Hear
Шурбо	Shurbo	Soup
Шӯхӣ кардан	Shukhi kardan	Joke

Э

Эскалатор	Eskalator	Escalator

Ю

Юбка	Yubka	Skirt

Я

Як	Yak	One
Як бор	Yak bor	Once
Як тарафа	Yak tarafa	One-way
Якрав	Yakrav	Stubborn
Якум	Yakum	First
Якхела	Yakkhela	Same

Tajik	Pronunciation	English
Якчанд	Yakchand	Few
Якчанд	Yakchand	Several
Якчоя	Yakjoya	Together
Ях	Yakh	Ice
Яхдон	Yakhdon	Fridge
Яхдон	Yakhdon	Refrigerator
Яхмос	Yakhmos	Ice cream

14483075R00070

Printed in Germany
by Amazon Distribution
GmbH, Leipzig